What Really Happened?

What Really Happened?

———

Thirteen Forgotten Mysteries of the Past

Harry M Bobonich and Chris Bobonich

ISBN-13: 9781542343763
ISBN-10: 1542343763

Contents

Also by Chris Bobonich

Plato's Utopia Recast: His Later Ethics and Politics (Oxford)

Plato's Laws: A Critical Guide (Cambridge), editor and contributor

Bloody Ivy: 13 Unsolved Campus Murders

Gone, Just Gone: Thirteen Baffling Disappearances

Also by Harry M. Bobonich

Seeing Around Corners: How Creative People Think

Big Mine Run: Recollections of the Coal Region

World War II: Memories of a GI

The Great Depression: Hard Times in the Coal Region

Pathfinders and Pioneers; Women in Science, Math & Medicine

Bloody Ivy: 13 Unsolved Campus Murders

Gone, Just Gone: Thirteen Baffling Disappearances

For Gloria

Introduction

In our first book, *Bloody Ivy*, we wrote about thirteen chilling unsolved murders on college campuses. Our next book, *Gone, Just Gone*, is a collection of thirteen baffling disappearances of men and women who vanished and never came back. In both books, we give our own view about what really happened.

In this book, we have decided to venture more broadly into the realm of the mysterious. We include some unsolved deaths and a disappearance, but we have also chosen some other tantalizing and mysterious tales. What they have in common is that we found them fascinating and want to know the real story. We hope that you, our readers, will enjoy them too.

A Watery Grave

Police divers discovered a woman's body deep down in a mammoth concrete tank filled with a million gallons of bitterly cold water. Someone had choked her until she lost consciousness and then quickly shoved her body into the massive tank where she drowned. The crime scene and her freezing body revealed nothing.

There was not one solitary shred of evidence to examine. No witnesses, no surveillance cameras, no weapon, no DNA, and no motive. It was a prototypical, clueless case like one that might be solved by Sherlock Holmes—and a modern twist on the classic Holmes "The Adventure of the Empty House" murder.

On the last day of her life, February 8, 2005, Geetha Angara took a coffee break around 9:30 a.m. Michael Irvolino, a colleague and coworker, said that Geetha "was laughing and smiling as usual." She was, however, in the company of a killer—but she didn't know it. Geetha was last seen at approximately 10:15 a.m., when she headed down to a lower-level basement at the water-treatment plant where she worked. She had less than two hours to live.

Geetha had not returned to her laboratory by noon, which was strange, and no one recalled seeing her since earlier that morning. When her work shift was over, staff members noted that her car was still in the company parking lot. A search of the plant revealed nothing, and she had not returned home. Plant officials finally called the local police around 11:20 p.m.

Why was Geetha, a brilliant chemist and mother of three, horribly murdered around midmorning at the plant where she worked? Who did it? The investigation would show it was one of her coworkers—but could we ever know which one?

Background

Geetha Angara was born in Madras, India. She earned a bachelor's degree and a master's degree in chemistry and graduated with honors. After arriving in the United States in 1984, she earned a second master's degree and a PhD in chemistry from New York University.

She was a senior chemist at the Passaic Valley Water Commission (PVWC) water-treatment plant in Totowa, New Jersey, about twelve miles northeast of Newark. The plant purified about eighty million gallons of drinking water daily for approximately eight hundred thousand customers. Geetha, who was recently promoted, was responsible for maintaining the quality of water to meet the standards set by the Environmental Protection Agency (EPA).

She was an exemplary employee, dedicated to her work and very conscious of her responsibility. She was described as energetic, efficient, and highly motivated to do well.

Geetha was five feet five inches tall and weighed 175 pounds. Her husband, Jaya, age fifty-one, was a banker. They had three children, whose ages were nine, thirteen, and nineteen. She was family oriented and a loving and caring mom. There was nothing in her life that suggested someone would want to harm her—but someone did.

Geetha Angara

Geetha's Strange Disappearance

During the 9:30 coffee break that cold February morning, a coworker mentioned to Geetha that two water filters in the basement area needed to be recalibrated. Other employees present said that they recalled Geetha saying that she would take care of it.

About a half hour later, she was seen carrying an oxygen canister to the ozone laboratory. Around 10:15 a.m., that very same coworker saw Geetha carrying her radio, clipboard, and a glass beaker as she descended into the concrete basement to attend to the water filters. Although it was an isolated area, it was not unfamiliar to Geetha; she had been down there many times, testing and taking readings at the mammoth water tank.

The photo shows workers walking through a tunnel at the PVWC treatment plant. The tunnel is similar to the one that Geetha also walked through when she disappeared.

At approximately 10:46 a.m., that same coworker reported to his supervisor that he found pieces of a broken glass beaker in the vicinity of the tank where Geetha had apparently been working earlier. Later, that coworker continued to ask other employees if anyone had seen Geetha.

It turned out that no one recalled seeing her since she went down to the basement—which was very weird.

Within a short period of about thirty minutes, Geetha, who had been all alone in that isolated area, seemed to just disappear. When the staff began looking for her, they noticed that her sandwich was still on her desk, so she clearly had not returned for lunch. After completing a thorough search of the plant, they were baffled to find that there was no trace of her.

Earlier, she had arranged to take her daughter to a basketball game that afternoon, but Geetha did not show up. It was unusual and perplexing to her family since she was always punctual. Moreover, she was not at home when her husband Jaya returned from work at 6:15 p.m.

At approximately 9:20 p.m., Jaya received a call from one of Geetha's coworkers, who said, "Her car was still in the parking lot and no one could find her." Finally, around 11:20 p.m., the plant officials notified the local police. By that time, Geetha had been missing for about thirteen hours. While it's understandable that people have accidents while at work, it is difficult to comprehend how anyone can vanish while on the job in the middle of the day (True Crime Diary 2006).

The Gruesome Killing

The next day following her disappearance, police divers discovered Geetha's radio and clipboard at the bottom of the thirty-five-foot-deep tank, which was filled with millions of gallons of freezing cold water. The massive tank was accessible only through a four-foot-wide opening at the top that was covered with a fifty-pound aluminum panel. Several hours later, divers finally found Geetha's dead body, which had drifted from the large tank to a secondary tank.

> The Prosecutor's Office began investigating the death as a homicide after five state medical examiners concluded that "deep muscle injuries" around [Geetha] Angara's neck arose from an assault, said John Latoracca, chief assistant prosecutor for

Passaic Co. They also found that she was unconscious when she fell into the water. (Crouse and Maddux 2009)

An autopsy showed that [Geetha] Angara had been forcibly subdued but that she was still alive when she fell, or was pushed into the tank. "There was no way out," said Passaic County prosecutor James Avigliano. "The water level was five feet below the opening. It was pitch-dark, ice-cold, thirty-six-degree water. There were no ladders. It was just a horrible way to die. There is no doubt that this is homicide." (Prud'Homme 2012)

Geetha's body was found fully clothed, and there was no indication that she was sexually molested. But who ended her life, and why?

The Investigation

The water-treatment plant was clearly protected from outside intruders. It had security guards and video cameras, and access to the plant was restricted. It was virtually impossible for an outsider to slip into the plant and carry out such a despicable crime in an isolated area and then leave undetected. Furthermore, security records showed that no unauthorized persons were present inside the plant during the time that Geetha was murdered.

Investigators ruled out the possibility of accidental death or suicide, since the fifty-pound aluminum plate on top of the tank, which is normally secured, was found slightly off to one side. Someone had to remove the bolts on the plate earlier so that he or she only had to slide the panel aside after rendering Geetha unconscious and then shoving her into the tank. The killer apparently did not take the time to completely replace the panel over the opening since he or she left the scene in a hurry.

There was no way that Geetha could have removed the panel cover and accidentally or voluntarily entered the water and then replaced the fifty-pound cover because the water level was five feet below the opening. Moreover, autopsy reports showed that she had been strangled.

By the time Geetha's body was discovered, the searchers at the plant had compromised the crime scene. The scattered pieces of the shattered glass beaker had been swept up and tossed in the trash. Furthermore, the water in the tank washed away any DNA evidence that might have been found on her body. The detectives found nothing.

Possible Motives

The investigators were not able to come up with any clear motive for the murder. Michael Irvolino, a colleague, said, "She was one of the sweetest people you could have hope [sic] to meet." Apparently, though, she was not popular with everyone at the plant. Since Geetha had recently been promoted, there was speculation by some that professional jealousy was a factor in her death. After her promotion, one employee said, "A lot of people were jealous. A lot of people didn't like her because she had a doctorate." But people don't go around murdering someone just because he or she was promoted. Another colleague said that there was "some racial prejudice. Ninety-eight percent of the plant is white, not all of them like seeing immigrants do well." Detectives, however, said that they were unable to find any evidence of a workplace grudge (Tresniowski 2006).

Geetha was responsible for making sure that the drinking water at the plant met the EPA standards so that it was safe to drink for almost one million customers. So why would anyone want to kill a respected employee like Geetha? After all, she has an important job to do, and she did it superbly.

Geetha's husband and one of her sisters, Saranya Rao, said that a week before Geetha was murdered she was home due to an illness. During that time, the water at the plant had turned a slight pink color. When Geetha returned to work, she was asked to retrain some of the workers on how such problems should be handled. Geetha's relatives wondered if that had anything to do with her death.

It is interesting to note that the EPA was concerned and sent in their investigators to the plant to check their maintenance records. State prosecutors tended to minimize the inspections by the EPA team, stating that federal agents "were just dotting their i's and crossing their t's. They found nothing." ("The Lady in the Passaic Valley Water Tank" 2012). Was it possible, however, that her murder did have something to do with the quality of water at the plant?

Geetha was very conscientiousness and always tried to do the right thing. Did she perhaps happen to see some illegal activity going on at the plant? And was she planning on blowing the whistle on a colleague? Keep in mind that she was not willing to compromise her integrity, and maybe that did not go over very well with some people.

One conspiracy-minded employee felt that the New Jersey mob was riled when PVWC changed from using chlorine to using ozone to treat their drinking water, since the switch curtailed work that was normally done by mob-controlled contractors. Geetha, on the other hand, was pleased and supported the decision when the plant officials decided to change over to the new ozone disinfectant system. How likely is it that someone was assigned to put a hit on Geetha? Hmm...There is no evidence, however, to support this theory ("The Lady in the Passaic Valley Water Tank" 2012).

Seeking the Killer

Since the investigators could not find an obvious motive for Geetha's murder, and the plant was secured from outside intruders, they concentrated their attention on all of the eighty-five employees at the plant. The fifty employees who were on duty the day of the killing were interviewed, and they also provided DNA samples. After further investigation, the authorities focused on eight employees who were deemed "people of special interest."

Finally they were down to three workers who were "people of real interest." Their stories were not consistent, and there was no hard evidence or a confession. All three suspects were asked to take a lie detector test. The police reported that one passed, one was inconclusive, and one refused to take the test. According to James Wood of the Passaic County prosecutor's office, one of the three is a supervisor and another is the coworker who reported finding the broken pieces of the glass beaker (Tresniowski 2006).

> One of the three suspects is the coworker who told [Geetha] Angara that two water filters needed to be calibrated. This same coworker was the last to see [Geetha] Angara as she descended into the lower level to calibrate the filters. This same man reported finding shards of glass from what turned out to be [Geetha] Angara's shattered beaker. And, according to coworkers, he was the first to notice [Geetha] Angara missing, asking repeatedly throughout the day if anyone had seen her. Mark Muller of *Newark's Star-Ledger* reports that Lt. James Wood…said detectives have a "good idea" of who killed [Geetha] Angara but don't have enough evidence for a charge to hold up in court. (True Crime Diary 2006)

By 2006, the investigation stalled since there was no definite motive and proof of a crime. While the case was technically open, no full-time detectives were working on the case. Geetha's husband and three children were beyond pain and totally frustrated.

> [In 2007] the Angara family filed a wrongful-death suit against the PVWC and a number of individually named supervisors and lab technicians, claiming the water plant—which had a history of accidents involving extremely high levels of chlorine in the water, open and unguarded water tanks, dirty work places, a lack of internal security measures, and a record of fifty-five health and safety violations—was a dangerous workplace that the PVWC allegedly knew about but failed to correct. (Prud'Homme 2012)

In 2008, Mark Mueller wrote:

> There's absolutely no question in my mind, said retired Lt. James Wood, who spent 18 months overseeing the probe as chief of

homicide in the Passaic County Prosecutor's Office. This is a horrible accident, but that's all it is—a tragic accident.

Wood said he believes another employee forgot to close the panel leading to the tank after gathering water samples and that [Geetha] Angara, carrying a clipboard and a beaker through the dark passageway, likely never noticed it was open.

The former detective said he was swayed in part by the research of a Scottish pathologist, Derrick Pounder, who has written that in a small percentage of cold-water drownings, a victim's neck, face and eyes develop marks resembling those in strangulation cases. The tank's water temperature was 36 degrees. (Mueller 2008)

In 2009, a state judge instructed attorneys to mediate the lawsuit. The commission's lawyer declined to comment, other than to say, "The PVWC continues to deny these unproven allegations." ("The Lady in the Passaic Valley Water Tank" 2012)

All three suspects continue to work at PVWC. The Angara family has asked the prosecutor's office for more assistance and also has appealed to the US attorney's office and state attorney general's office to look into Geetha's murder. Unfortunately, the case has gone cold.

A Scenario for Geetha's Murder

What makes this murder even more puzzling from the beginning is that the authorities knew exactly where to find the killer. The problem, as it turned out, is that no one was talking. While it appeared that Geetha didn't have any enemies—and there was no reason why she should—someone wanted her dead.

Geetha apparently was not apprehensive about carrying out a routine calibration of some water filters, even though it was in a lower-level, isolated concrete basement. After all, it was in the middle of the morning and there were about fifty other employees at work that day. Geetha, however, was alone in that remote area.

Since she was totally unaware of any danger, and hence defenseless, her killer had the advantage of a surprise attack. The timeline was narrow and the murderer had to act fast—it was all carried out quickly. As Geetha was going about her normal work duties that morning, a trusted coworker attacked her from behind and choked her until she lost consciousness.

He might have used only his bare hands, but it's more likely he had a thin rope, which he used to perfection to choke her more easily and swiftly. The deep muscle injuries around her neck were an indication of how forcibly she had been subdued.

The killer quickly pushed the fifty-pound panel aside and shoved her down into the massive thirty-five-foot-deep tank where she drowned. The slayer then tossed her phone and clipboard into the tank but did not bother to deal with the pieces of scattered glass from the broken beaker.

The vicious, cowardly murderer made a mistake by leaving the panel slightly askew and quickly hurried away. The murderer left Geetha in that pitch-dark tank to die in a million gallons of ice-cold water and brazenly continued with his normal workday. Geetha's frozen body, which meanwhile had drifted into an adjacent tank, was discovered the following day.

One can only shudder to think of how nightmarish her feelings must have been when she realized that a trusted worker was attacking her. It's likely that she didn't have time to cry out, but even if she did, her muffled cries probably would not have been heard. It's hard to imagine a more dreadful way to die.

The tank was accessible only through a four-foot-wide opening that was covered with a fifty-pound aluminum panel, which is normally secured with bolts. Since the killer didn't have time to remove the bolts and then push the panel aside after subduing Geetha, someone had to take out the bolts earlier and only had to slide the panel off to one side and then shove her into the tank. The trusted coworker may not have carried out the heinous crime all alone since there were too many mysterious circumstances surrounding her death.

We think it was a combination of factors that led to her demise, rather than just one clear motive. Geetha took her job seriously and was dedicated to maintaining the EPA standards regarding the quality of the drinking water. If she saw someone doing something wrong, she would confront him or her, but she would do so in a civil manner.

Some employees, however, resented her recent promotion, status, and professional competency. Undoubtedly, there were also some who felt threatened by her important position at the plant. And it's also likely that there were some employees who harbored a grudge in seeing a minority woman achieving success.

Jealous people, however, can often mask their rancor, but over time their bitterness and resentment can possibly result in murder. And sometimes they will even carry out their evil crimes without fear of retribution.

In summary, we think that: (a) Geetha was set up to go down to the isolated basement area, (b) someone removed the bolts from the panel prior to the attack on her, (c) the crime scene was completely compromised, (d) the delay in thoroughly searching for Geetha was inexcusable and perhaps deliberate, and (e) the long time it took for plant officials to notify the police was questionable and suspicious—all suggest that it was a planned killing carried out by a trusted coworker with the help of another person in a supervisory capacity.

Aftermath

"A decade has now gone by since the murder, and I'm happy to help put a spotlight on this," State Senator Joe Kyrillos said. "So I'll be asking acting Attorney General John Hoffman to review this case, to find a way for his office to re-engage" (Mueller 2015).

We agree: it's never too late in such a tragic case as this to take a new look at evidence, witnesses, and suspects.

The Uranium Bath

It all started so innocently on a hot, humid Sunday night on June 17, 1984. It was close to midnight when Dave Bocks arrived at the sprawling nuclear plant in the small rural town of Fernald, Ohio, where he was employed. The nuclear facility was engulfed in a dense fog that night, which not only covered the Fernald area but also gave it an eerie look. Was it an omen?

In that year, Ronald Reagan, fortieth president of the United States, was reelected for a second term and Apple Computer released the Macintosh personal computer. Movie fans were enjoying *Ghostbusters*, *Indiana Jones and the Temple of Doom* and *Terminator*: others were listening to "Say, say, say" and "When Doves Cry."

For the next several hours, Dave was given job assignments at various locations at the plant. He took a break at 4:00 a.m., which is the lunch hour on the graveyard shift; but then, just one hour later around 5:00 a.m., he was just gone. Dave never made it through the night; somehow, he mysteriously disappeared. But how does someone just vanish while at work?

At around 7:30 that morning, the furnace operator at Plant 6 reported to his supervisor that he noticed a strange odor, and also that the temperature in the furnace dropped unexpectedly for a brief period of time. His supervisor told him that he found nothing wrong and to proceed with his work as usual.

Further investigations, however, revealed that the temperature drop indicated that something foreign might have been dumped into the furnace. When the plant officials discovered an unusual sticky coating on top of the oven and also a bone fragment, they called in the authorities.

It took several days for the furnace to cool down. When the oven was cleaned out, the investigators found Dave's keys, some human bones, remnants of a walkie-talkie, a wire frame from safety glasses, and steel toes from safety shoes along with metal shoe eyelets and button fasteners from workmen's coveralls.

Apparently Dave's body had been incinerated: but how did his body end up in the super hot furnace? Was it an accident? Was it murder, or something else?

Investigators were unable to determine how Dave could have entered the furnace. They suggested that he might have committed suicide since he had a history of psychological problems.

His family and investigative reporter D. C. Cole, however, believe that he was murdered by some who suspected that he was a potential whistle-blower: he knew too much.

The nuclear plant's dirty secret was that they had been releasing enormous amounts of radioactive dust particles into the atmosphere for years. Did that have anything to do with Dave's demise?

Background

Dave Bocks

Dave Bocks was born on November 4, 1944, in Staten Island, New York. His family eventually moved to the small town of Loveland, Ohio. Dave graduated from Loveland High School in 1963, and the following year he started taking night courses in industrial management at the University of Cincinnati.

In 1965, Dave got married at the age of twenty: he and Carline had three children. Dave, however, had a serious drinking problem and ended up being an alcoholic by age thirty-two. He was admitted to the hospital and then transferred to a psychiatric ward. Dave was discharged in January 1977, and the following month he and his wife were divorced.

Dave was hospitalized for a short period in 1979, which appears to have been related to the death of his mother. After being discharged, he was on medication since he was prone to anxiety attacks. He appeared to be doing well and returned to work. Dave, however, was hospitalized a third time for just a short stay because he was very nervous and also depressed.

Dave's medical records indicated that he suffered from a "schizophrenic reaction"; however, upon further review he was apparently suffering from a post-traumatic stress disorder. By 1980, at age thirty-five, Dave appeared to be doing better and had a more positive view about his life and the future.

In 1981, Dave was hired as a pipe fitter at the Feed Materials Production Center (FMPC), located in the small rural town of Fernald, about twenty miles northwest of Cincinnati, Ohio. Charles Shouse, his former supervisor, said, "Bocks got along well with people and that he was a good worker." Dave also earned the respect and trust of his coworkers.

FMPC was a secret nuclear weapons facility that was owned by the Department of Energy (DOE) and operated by National Lead of Ohio (NLO). NLO converted uranium ore into metal and then fabricated the metal uranium into cores for the Atomic Energy Commission's (AEC's) plutonium reactors at various locations across the country.

Fernald Feed Materials Production Center

Dave's Bizarre Disappearance

On Sunday night, June 17, Dave Bocks met Harry Easterling, his co-worker, in the parking lot of a nearby restaurant where they alternated days driving each other from the restaurant to work. Dave got into Easterling's truck, and they drove to the nuclear plant where they both were employed. The conversation between the two men appeared to be normal.

When they arrived at the plant, Dave reported to the maintenance section for his work assignment. It was a typical workday: Dave opened his toolbox and placed his keys and lock on top, and he went to one plant, while Easterling worked in another area. The large spread-out nuclear facility was comprised of various plants, which were designated by number.

Dave's duties at the facility were to inspect and maintain the safety pumps and dust collectors employed in processing the uranium. He was aware of the dangers working at the plant, and at times he would warn Easterling of potentially hazardous situations.

In the fall of that year, NLO accidentally released vast amounts of uranium dust into the atmosphere, resulting in radioactive contamination of the surrounding area. Furthermore, an investigation revealed that NLO had released over two hundred tons of radioactive dust particles into the atmosphere over a period of years. We will have more to say on this subject later.

According to his supervisor, Charles Shouse, Dave worked at a number of different plants that Monday morning. From 12:30 to 2:00 a.m., Dave worked at Plant 1. Around 2:00 a.m., Shouse said he transported Dave in the company pickup truck from Plant 1 to Plant 4. The facility covered so much ground that workers often used a vehicle to get from one plant to another.

Shortly afterward, a worker stated that he saw Dave and Shouse sitting in a parked pickup truck. They seemed to be having a serious discussion; however, even though it was a hot night, the windows were rolled up on the truck.

Dave then worked at Plant 8 from 2:30 to 4:00 a.m., when he took his lunch break with Easterling and Shouse. The last time Easterling saw Dave was shortly after lunchtime. Shouse said the last time he saw Dave was about 5:00 a.m. outside Plant 4. After that, Dave seemed to have disappeared.

At around 7:00 a.m., there was a safety meeting in Plant 4, but Dave was absent. Afterward, when Easterling went to the maintenance building to put his tools away, he noticed that Dave's toolbox was still open, so he thought that he might be working overtime. He inquired about Dave but could not locate him. Easterling informed the security guard at the desk that he had to leave for home, but he would meet Dave at the restaurant as usual for the next workday.

Meanwhile, at around 7:30 that Monday morning, the furnace operator in Plant 6 reported that something unusual occurred in his oven: the inside was covered with a tacky substance that had a bad odor. Plant records showed that at 5:10 that morning, the temperature in the furnace in Plant 6 dropped twenty-eight degrees for a short period of time, indicating that something foreign had entered the furnace.

The furnace or vat, also referred to as the salt bath furnace, held nine hundred gallons of molten salt, which served as a metallurgical heat treatment process for the uranium ingots. The vat was ten feet eight inches long, four feet high, and three feet wide.

On the next workday, Easterling arrived at the restaurant as usual, which was late Monday night, but Dave did not show up; however, his car was still in the parking lot. Easterling then happened to touch the hood of Dave's car and noticed that it was cold as if it had not been driven recently. Easterling became concerned about Dave and reported him missing when he arrived at the plant. Since it was about nineteen hours ago that Dave had disappeared, they began a search inside the complex facility ("Dave Bocks: When a Nuclear Plant Employee's Remains Are Found in the Plant Furnace, Some Say It Was Suicide, Others Murder").

The Investigation

On Tuesday, June 19, Robert W. Lippincott, chief of Fire and Safety at NLO, said that the Security Department then opened Dave's two lockers. They found that his street clothing and wallet were still in his street-clothing locker; however, his plant-clothing locker was empty, which indicated that Dave did not leave the facility earlier with Easterling when he went home the previous day. Also, Dave's car was still in the parking lot at the restaurant where he always met with Easterling. Early on, some thought that Dave might have secretly left the plant without telling anyone and planned on leaving everything and everyone behind; but clearly that was not the case.

Meanwhile, when the plant officials looked more closely at the sticky residue around the furnace at Plant 6, they found a piece of bone that resembled a human collar bone. The test results from the laboratory concluded that the material had some characteristics similar to human bone. The authorities were notified and the furnace was shut down, but it took several days for the furnace to cool sufficiently before anyone could enter it safely.

It wasn't until Saturday, June 23, that detective Peter Alderucci of the Hamilton County Sheriff's Department was lowered into the furnace.

When Alderucci searched the furnace, he found: Dave's keys, walkie-talkie parts, radio batteries (Dave always carried his radio on the job), fragments of human bones, steel toes from safety shoes, part of a wire frame from safety glasses, a fragment of a radiation tag, shoe eyelets, metal fasteners from coveralls, and some stainless steel wire.

According to former chief of police Victor Carrelli, "The keys belonged to the victim's car. They also belonged to three padlocks of his, and one key we believed went into his residence but we couldn't prove that because it was bent and not [in a] very good shape."

But how was security able to open the lock on Dave's street-clothing locker? Detective Peter Alderucci of the Hamilton County Sheriff's Department stated that photographic evidence showed that his lock had not been cut open or damaged.

Furthermore, Easterling said, "When I left the plant to go over to the maintenance shop, his keys were in the box. When I left there, to go home, they were still in the box. I then went home. When I came back that night, his keys were still in the top of his toolbox. The supervisor closed his box, put the lock on his toolbox and took his keys out of the box. And from there on I do not know what happened to the keys."

But how did Dave end up in the incredibly hot furnace? Did he enter voluntarily? Or did some, who felt he knew too much, shove him into that fiery abyss?

Carrelli said they were unable to find any evidence to show that Dave was murdered. Since Dave had a history of psychological problems, the investigators suggested that he might have committed suicide.

According to Detective Alderucci, Dave weighed about two hundred pounds, and when his body entered the furnace that was 1350 degrees Fahrenheit, his body would have exploded, since a human body contains a considerable amount of water. (The average human body contains about 65 percent water.) It's similar to tossing an apple into the furnace, which workers sometimes did: the apple, like anything that contains water, exploded.

There is always an opening of about 9 × 22 inches at the top of the furnace to vent off heat. If Dave attempted to enter the extremely hot furnace feet first, the upper part of his body most likely would have landed outside the furnace. And if he entered head first, the lower part of his body would probably fall outside the furnace since the opening is so small.

The Hamilton County Sheriff's office maintained that Dave placed a ladder next to the furnace before "getting a running jump, squatting down and diving in" through the small opening at the top of the furnace. We find this simply unbelievable.

A detailed letter from Dr. Robert Baker, professor of psychology at the University of Kentucky, strongly suggests that Dave did not commit suicide by entering the furnace on his own: "it is almost inconceivable that he would take this unusual and highly improbable way."

Nevertheless, the investigators and plant officials were basically in agreement that Dave had committed suicide. On the Certificate of Death for Dave Bocks, Coroner Frank Cleveland, wrote: "cause and manner of death undetermined" (D.C. Cole 1988).

Other Opinions

Casey Drake, Dave's daughter, stated that her father did not commit suicide. She pointed out that he was planning to go on a vacation to Florida with her and his brother. Others, including family members, felt strongly that he had been murdered and possibly was still conscious when he was lowered into the furnace.

It is significant to note that D. C. Cole, investigative reporter, also thought Dave might have been murdered. Cole wrote:

> I think he knew something. It's possible that he was a whistle blower or was going to be a whistle blower. Plant 8 had released four times more radioactive contaminants into the environment than any other plant at the plant site. I believe that they could have shot him, or they could have hit him with something and knocked him unconscious. They took the body to Plant 6, where the furnace is. I would hate to think that he was conscious. I can't imagine a more horrible death than that. ("Dave Bocks:

When a Nuclear Plant Employee's Remains Are Found in the Plant Furnace, Some Say It Was Suicide, Others Murder" (D.C. Cole 1988).

NLO was closed five years after Dave death. There was no normal burial for him: his scanty remains were so radioactive that they were sealed in a container and shipped to Nevada, where they were stored with other toxic materials.

A Decade Later—The Letter

Casey Drake, Dave's daughter, received an anonymous twelve-page letter dated July 8, 1994, suggesting that Dave's death was due to foul play. Reporter Cole wrote: "Upon further investigation, the evidence would eventually reveal Robert M. Spenceley, former plant manager at Fernald, thought he could protect his identity by remaining anonymous. Surely, he did not believe anybody could ever figure out who wrote the letter since he didn't sign it, but he was wrong."

We will summarize the main points in Spenceley's letter in this section and also adapt some of his comments for our conclusion. Spenceley wrote:

"My conscious [sic] has kept me awake for many nights. I have dreaded the moment when I would write this letter to you. I still almost hope I won't send it. If anyone were to find out I would be ruined. Both publicly and privately."

"Don't ask any questions and don't make waves were the two unbreakable rules for employment," Casey is told. "These rules prove to be an impossibility for anyone with a conscious [sic]. Your father was one of those with a conscious [sic]," the FMPC plant manager reminded Casey.

"Your father was killed so that others would continue to receive a paycheck, the union would still retain their political power, NLO would retain their high dollar contract, and the DOE would retain their place as taxpayer rip-off artists. They just want everyone to shut up," Spenceley said, adding, "before someone really performs an investigation, which would mean their loss of power and money."

"The 'family' [management] does not want to believe that anyone employed at NLO would purposely kill another human being," Spenceley wrote. "If nothing else, preponderance of the evidence proves beyond a reasonable doubt that the DOE, FBI, NLO as well as the Hamilton County Sheriff's office and Coroner are all part of some organized crime family; with a long criminal history as horrible and gruesome as Bocks' death."

"What do I think?" Spenceley asked Casey. "I think I know too much already. But I can tell you what to do so that you may learn more about the truth," he said.

"His body was destroyed," Spenceley confesses, "to allow a major cover up to ensure that the U.S. Government was not revealed as the bureaucratic crime network that it was and still remains today."

The former Fernald plant manager wrote to Casey, "One true statement from anyone would have disrupted the government from the state of Ohio all the way through the United States of America." (Cole 1988)

Four years after the Spenceley letter came out, D. C. Cole, in his well-documented book, wrote:

The hard-core evidence clearly proves that the DOE, FBI, NLO, Butler and Hamilton County Sheriff's office were all secretly working together side by side. And the attorneys all knew the truth. Fifteen years later, now the rest of us are discovering the truth too.

They are the ones responsible for covering up the horrible, gruesome death of a thirty-nine year old pipefitter at the infamous FMPS nuclear weapons plant site in Fernald on Father's Day, June 17–18, back in 1984. (Cole 1988)

What Happened to Dave?

While Dave's death was mysterious, it wasn't a mystery. Let's examine his strange disappearance during the witching hour (when demons, witches, and ghosts are thought to appear) while working the graveyard shift at the Fernald nuclear facility.

Accident

Since Dave was not assigned to work at Plant 6, there was no reason for him to be there. Furthermore, he was not seen in that vicinity shortly before he disappeared. There is no reasonable way that Dave could have accidentally stumbled or slipped and fell into the narrow opening at the top of the vat at Plant 6, since he had to have a ladder or a wooden portable stairway to reach the top of the tank, even though it wasn't that high off the ground. Also, the vat opening was so small that he would have had to force himself down into the tank. We think it was physically impossible for him to accidentally fall into the vat.

Suicide

The authorities pointed out and made an issue of Dave's past medical history of mental problems and concluded that he most likely committed suicide by entering the furnace voluntarily. Dave, however, appeared to be well adjusted and doing good work at Fernald. There were no indications that he was upset or depressed; in fact, he was planning on going on a vacation soon.

We think it is very unlikely that he would have taken his own life. It would have been almost impossible for him to squeeze through that rather narrow opening (9 × 22 inches) at the top of the vat and become totally consumed without leaving part of his body on the outside. Detective Alderucci said, "It [the furnace] was so hot, you couldn't get close to it. We stood there with a fire suit on and still it was so hot that you couldn't stand to be near it for any more than 10 or 15 seconds."

The heat was so unbearable that if Dave tried to force himself through the small opening, he most likely would have been overcome and lost consciousness. On the other hand, if by some miracle he was able to get close enough to enter feet first, he would have lost both legs but the rest of his body would have been left behind. It wasn't a matter of just jumping off into a wide-open vat and then perishing instantaneously.

Murder

On Sunday, June 17, Dave and Easterling arrived at the nuclear facility shortly before midnight and then changed into their work clothes to begin their 12:00 midnight to 8:30 a.m. graveyard shift. They both headed over to Plant 12 to get their job assignments. Dave unloaded his toolbox and then placed his lock with the keys inside the top of the box.

Dave, who was responsible for inspecting and maintaining equipment throughout the complex facility, was specifically assigned to make sure the safety pumps and dust collectors that processed the uranium were working properly. He was assigned to Plant 8, which accepted waste from all the other plant sites: it was a wastewater-treatment plant. Dave said that it was very difficult to perform preventative maintenance on the pumps since they were in extremely poor condition, and that Plant 8 would have to be shut down for major repairs before it was safe for anyone to work there. Plant 8 played a critical role at the facility; if it were shut down, the entire Fernald complex of plants would also close down. In that case, there would be a major investigation, which most likely would end up closing the site permanently—and no one would have a job.

Around 4:30 Monday morning, an argument took place concerning safe working procedures: Dave was told that if he couldn't handle the job, he could quit. Dave was stubborn and had a reputation of not taking any "guff" from anyone, and pretty soon a physical fight started and Dave was injured. "When Dave got hurt the gig was up and explanations would have to be made," Spenceley explained in his letter to Dave's daughter. "Fighting and injuring a worker would get your security clearance revoked and you would never work on a DOE site again." We think that Dave knew too much about what was going on at the plant, and some thought that he was a potential whistle-blower.

The die was cast: Dave had to be eliminated. We think that Dave was knocked unconscious or to the point where he could not offer any resistance and transported to Plant 6. The overhead crane most likely was used to remove the heavy lid aside, and then Dave's body was lowered into the furnace. The crane then replaced the lid to its normal position. It is also possible that several employees wearing acid master suits (to protect themselves from the heat) could have shoved Dave into the furnace through the smaller opening that was 9 × 22 inches, which normally vented heat from the furnace, but we think this is less likely.

On June 18th Monday morning, the furnace temperature in Plant 6 dropped twenty-eight degrees (1350 to 1322) for approximately fifteen minutes at 5:10, and then it returned to the normal operating temperature of 1350 degrees Fahrenheit. Chief of Fire and Safety Lippincott, however, wrote on Monday, June 18, that at 2:07 a.m., there was a fifty-minute long temperature drop of sixty-two degrees (1350 to 1288) in the furnace at Plant 6.

It is important to note that the temperature chart only showed the time between the hours of 3:00 a.m. and 7:00 a.m., which showed the twenty-eight-degree drop in temperature. Attorney Martin asked why wasn't there a plant chart record of the sixty-two-degree-drop in temperature at 2:07 a.m.? Supervisor Shouse told Attorney Martin that on least two occasions that morning—once at around 3:00 a.m. and also at 7:00 a.m.—a worker had to "adjust the tape on the furnace." The missing chart, which normally would have recorded what happened at 2:07 a.m., is suspicious to say the least.

It is of interest to note that Daniel B. Katz, an NLO engineer, who also investigated Dave's death, calculated that a man of Dave's weight (about two hundred pounds) would cause a drop of sixty degrees (1350 to 1288) if he were dropped into the furnace in Plant 6. So the calculation from Katz matched the drop of sixty-two degrees reported by Lippincott at 2:07 a.m.

Spenceley suggested in his letter that the initial twenty-eight-degree temperature drop at 5:07 a.m. was "rigged" and reflected the insertion of an ingot into the furnace. If a human were lowered into the furnace, it would have required a longer period of time to return back to the 1350-degree mark. Spenceley added that furnace records revealed that when wet ingots are inserted in the furnace, the recovery time (temperature drop) is much shorter than it would be for a human body, which contains much more water. The evidence seems to indicate that Dave entered the furnace at 2:07 a.m. and not at 5:10 a.m. Furthermore detective Alderucci stated that they found an ingot in the furnace when it was searched on Saturday, June 23.

Dave's time card was also "fixed" to make it appear that he clocked and left the facility at 8:15 a.m. on Monday morning on June 18 and also at 8:15 a.m. on Tuesday morning on June 19. Dave's body was inside the furnace hours before his normal departure time of 8:15 a.m., on Monday, June 18. During the investigation, Easterling said it was a common practice to punch each other's time card, which he did in this case. In a 1992 interview, however, he denied punching Dave's card but stated that he was asked to do so.

Furthermore, Spenceley was curious why Easterling concluded that Dave was missing because his car at the restaurant parking lot was cool. He also wondered why Easterling seemed nervous and was the only one who asked the authorities if there were any suspects after they found his coworker's items in the furnace. After Easterling told the supervisor about Dave's keys on his toolbox, they were then placed in the supervisor's desk. Spenceley stated that Easterling took the keys and threw them into the furnace at Plant 6 to cast suspicion away from himself. According to Spenceley, the supervisor would have turned in the keys to security, but Easterling didn't think about that.

The evidence is clear: Dave was a potential whistle-blower who knew too much, and he had to be eliminated. We agree with D. C. Cole's theory, which he details in his excellent book, that there was a conspiracy: Dave Bocks was murdered. But large conspiracies are hard to hide, and no more than one or two people need have been involved. The inquiries afterward may have been slipshod, not because the investigators were part of the conspiracy but just because they may not have wanted to discover the full truth.

Aftermath

From 1951 to 1989 the nuclear plant at Ferndale produced almost 70 percent of all uranium used in our nation's nuclear weapons. There were, however, denials and a false awareness by plant authorities over the years that turned out to be a big deception regarding the safety of workers and residents in the area. In 1988, while the facility was still in operation, the following (from a lengthier article) appeared in *The New York Times*.

> Government officials overseeing a nuclear plant in Ohio knew for decades that they were releasing thousands of tons of radioactive uranium waste into the environment, exposing thousands of workers and residents in the region, a Congressional panel said today.
>
> The 37-year-old plant at Fernald, Ohio, near Cincinnati, processes uranium for use in nuclear weapons and in the Energy Department's military reactors in South Carolina and elsewhere. The plant has been closed since last Friday by a strike over wages and safety, and amid mounting concern over environmental and safety problems; the department has recently closed two other plants in its warhead production system. (Noble 1988)

And from the *Chicago Tribune*:

> In 1988, Richard Celeste, Governor of Ohio, also spoke out, "accusing the federal government of 'deceit and mismanagement' called on President Reagan Tuesday to shut down the Fernald nuclear weapons plant until steps can be taken to contain radioactive wastes that have been entering the region's air and water for the past three decades." (Thom 1988)

In 1989, the Fernald facility stopped production of uranium and the plant was closed. It was just one of a number of other plants that were added to a list of Superfund cleanup sites. It took the Department of Energy fourteen years to finally clean up the badly contaminated site. In

2008, the former nuclear plant is now called the Fernald Preserve. The nature preserve is opened to visitors and tourists.

Reporter Ralph Vartabedian wrote:

> Contrary to appearances, there is nothing natural here. The high ground is filled with radioactive debris, scooped from the soil around a former uranium foundry that produced crucial parts for the reactor's nuclear weapons program.
>
> A $4.4 billion cleanup transformed Fernald from a dangerous contaminated factory complex into an environmental showcase. But it is "clean" only by terms of a legal agreement. Its soils contain many times the natural amounts of radioactivity, and a plume of tainted water extends underground about a mile. Nobody can ever safely live here, federal scientists say, and the site will have to be monitored eventually forever. (Vartabedian 2009)

In 1994, a class-action lawsuit brought by former Fernald workers ended with a financial settlement. In addition, the settlement provided for a lifelong medical monitoring for the workers.

On the night of November 13, 1974, Karen Silkwood, another nuclear plant worker, was killed in a car crash on her way to deliver a manila folder to a *New York Times* reporter: the folder contained alleged health and safety violations at the Kerr-McGee nuclear plant in Oklahoma where she worked. The manila folder was never found. In his book, *The Whistleblowers's Dilemma: Snowden, Silkwood and Their Quest for the Truth*, author Richard Rashke wrote, "Karen Silkwood was run off the road and the FBI knows who did it to her." Thanks to the wonderful movie *Silkwood*, with Meryl Streep, everyone remembers Karen Silkwood. David Bocks, the Man in the Uranium Bath, has been forgotten. To paraphrase the brilliant Townes van Zandt song "Pancho and Lefty" (made famous by Willie Nelson): Karen needs your prayers; it's true, but save a few for Dave too.

Hot Acidic Bath

On June 7, 2016, Colin Scott and his sister Sable went on a college graduation trip to Yellowstone National Park. After walking around for some time, they decided to leave the boardwalk near Pork Chop Geyser in search of "hot pot"—a place where they could soak in one of the thermal springs.

After walking about two hundred feet up a small hill, they came to a steaming hot spring that apparently appealed to Colin. Even though visitors are not allowed to soak in any of the thermal features throughout the park, Colin proceeded to reach down and check the temperature of the hot pool, which was approximately six feet long, nine feet wide, and ten feet deep. As Sable was taking photos of her brother with her cell phone, he suddenly slipped and tumbled into the hot acidic spring. While she tried to save him, her desperate attempts were unsuccessful.

Later, search and rescue rangers noticed Scott's body floating in the steaming thermal pool: they were unable to recover his body due to a lightning storm in the area. The following day, however, searchers were not able to find his body. Deputy Chief Ranger Lorant Veress said, "In very short order, there was a significant amount of dissolving"—the hot acid had consumed Colin's body. It appeared that he just seemed to vanish.

While there are warning signs reminding people of the dangers of the park's hot springs, as well as venturing off-trail, people often get adventuresome and break the rules: and that at times results in fatalities.

In our previous story, the body of Dave Bocks was vaporized in a superhot uranium bath. And in this story, Colin Sable's body was apparently completely dissolved in the very hot acidic spring. In a way, they both seemed to eventually vanish into thin air.

Ashley's Last Night Out

It was pitch dark and bitter cold very early in the morning on February 10, 1999, when a motorist suddenly spotted what appeared to be a human body lying in the middle of the road.

No one pulled a trigger on a gun; no one brandished a pointed dagger and then stabbed the victim to death. A pair of strong hands of a cruel killer that touched life and then shortly afterward felt death had viciously strangled a young girl.

The day before, fifteen-year-old Ashley Ouellette had permission from her parents to spend the night with her girlfriend. It was, however, the last night of her very young life. Sometime later that night, Ashley then decided to leave the home of her girlfriend and go to the residence of Earl and Muriel Sanborn. Ashley had a relationship previously with Steven Sanborn, who was her former boyfriend and older brother of Daniel, who was Ashley's classmate at Thornton Academy. Ashley arrived at the Sanborn home around midnight.

But why did Ashley change her mind? Was it a secret she had in mind all along and kept it to herself? Or was it a spur-of-the-moment decision?

It was quite late when she arrived at the Sanborn residence; nevertheless, Ashley was allowed to spend the night with them. Around 12:30 a.m., Muriel made arrangements for Ashley to sleep on a couch in their home. She said it was the last time she saw Ashley.

But then, something terrible happened over the next several hours—and no one is talking. At 4:00 a.m., a passing motorist came upon Ashley's lifeless body lying in the middle of the road about ten miles from the Sanborn home.

Who murdered Ashley and why? And how did she end up where she was found? Her mysterious death has never been solved.

Background

Ashley Ouellette was born on March 29, 1983, in Saco, Maine, a beautiful New England coastal town, which is located in the southern part of the state.

In 1999, Ashley was a sophomore at Thornton Academy in Saco: it was the same high school her father had attended. In that same year, the US Senate acquitted President Bill Clinton after the House of Representatives impeached him for his sexual relationship with twenty-two-year-old Monica Lewinsky, who was an intern at the White House. Almost fifty million people watched Lewinsky's first TV interview with Barbara Walters. The second Woodstock festival was held in New York. John F. Kennedy Jr. was killed in a plane crash. The Blackberry phone was released, and the New York Yankees won their twenty-fifth World Series.

While Ashley was an all-around, fun-loving, great person, she was having some difficulty at school. At the time, she was not getting good grades in her studies and therefore was not permitted to stay overnight at her girlfriend's home during the week. But when her grades improved and she seemed to be doing better overall, her mother changed her mind even though she had a peculiar feeling that night—a mom's intuition? Unfortunately, it was a decision that led to Ashley's death.

Ashley Ouellette

What Happened to Ashley?

On Tuesday, February 9, 1999, Robert and Lise Ouellette allowed their daughter Ashley to spend the night at the home of her girlfriend Alia Page, who lived in downtown Saco, about a mile from Ashley's home.

Around 10:30 p.m. that night, Ashley called her parents for a brief chat and to say goodnight. It was the last time they would hear their daughter's voice—she only had several hours to live. Sometime before midnight, Ashley changed her mind and made a decision contrary to the arrangement she had with her parents and decided to leave the Page home and head off to the Sanborn residence.

Earl and Muriel Sanborn and their two sons were at home when Ashley arrived sometime around midnight. Did Ashley have a story about why she was visiting at such a late hour? In any event, the Sanborn parents agreed that Ashley could spend the night with them. Around 12:30 a.m., Muriel provided bedding for Ashley to sleep on a couch in the basement just outside of her two sons' bedrooms in the basement.

Around 4:00 a.m., a motorist driving on Pine Point Road in Scarborough noticed what appeared to be a body lying in the roadway. He quickly slowed down, then stopped his car, and cautiously walked over to take a closer look at the person. When he recognized that it was a young girl and that she appeared to be dead, he quickly called 911.

Someone had murdered Ashley and dumped her in the middle of the road several miles from the Sanborn home.

The Investigation

The motorist who made the horrific discovery told the authorities that Ashley's body was still warm and that there was some blood around her mouth and nose when he found her. Later, a closer examination revealed that Ashley had been strangled.

While Ashley had told her parents that she was going to spend the night at her friend's house, investigators said that she had instead attended a party with some friends. Shortly after calling her mom, several boys from her high school also arrived at the party. One of the boys,

Jay Carney, reportedly then drove some of the girls, including Ashley, to the Sanborn home. Not long after midnight, Ashley remained at the Sanborn home while the others left.

When the investigating team learned that Ashley was last seen at the Sanborn residence, they began to interview Earl and Muriel Sanborn and their two sons—Steven, who was 18, and Daniel, age 16.

Steven told the detectives that he went to school the next morning, Wednesday, where he heard students talking about a girl who was found dead, and that it might be Ashley. He also said that he had a sexual relationship with Ashley several years ago, according to an article in the *Bangor Daily News*, February 19, 1999.

Daniel, however, was inconsistent during his interview. He told the authorities that he saw Ashley early on Wednesday morning and that she asked to stay overnight at his home since she had an argument with her parents and they tossed her out. Daniel then told the police that he went off to school that morning; however, after contradicting himself, he recanted that comment and stated that he slept late and went to Old Orchard Beach with some friends that afternoon. The police began to focus on Daniel because of his suspicious behavior.

The police then obtained search warrants for the Sanborn home and also Daniel's car, which was an Eagle Summit. Inside the Sanborn home, they found a trail of blood droplets from the kitchen that led into the living room. The police took samples of carpet and upholstery along with bedding, jewelry, a stained pillow, and a condom. They also took clothing, hair, tissue samples, and fingernail clippings from Daniel.

From inside Daniel's vehicle, the authorities confiscated a black shirt, a gold ring, and a scarf, along with samples of hair and fingernail particles. They also found brown grass in his car that was similar to the brown grass discovered on Ashley's body.

Although the investigation appeared to be moving in a direction that was leading to a suspect, there were no arrests. Lieutenant Bob McDonough, of the Criminal Investigation Division of the Maine State Police felt that they had a good idea of what happened. He said, "I think we all are familiar with the Ashley Ouellette case, but we are just shy of being able to prove that case beyond a reasonable doubt." Sergeant Matthew Stewart, the lead investigator in the case, said, "They were unable to place Ashley alive outside the Sanborn residence."

The police had Ashley's body and they had some evidence, but they didn't have a motive. As a result, they were unable to prove their case beyond a reasonable doubt. Stewart said, "We believe there are people who have direct knowledge, solid knowledge about what happened to Ashley. We need people to come forward."

After four months of investigation, the police carried out over two hundred interviews. They tested and analyzed all the samples of evidence collected. Stewart said, "We're not yet at a point where we can reach standards of probable cause (for an arrest) on any one particular person at this particular time. It takes a lot of time and a lot of patience" (Katiesback 2002).

With all the evidence that the police had, it was not enough. And so, with no confession or statement, the case remained unsolved.

The Ouellettes Take Action

In February 2001, Robert and Lise Ouellette filed a wrongful death lawsuit against Earl and Muriel Sanborn. They maintained that the Sanborns owed Ashley "a duty of reasonable care including a duty to provide reasonably safe premises and a duty to reasonably supervise the activities of minors…in their home." The suit also alleged "Daniel Sanborn, now 18, assaulted Ouellette, injuring her in a way that ultimately caused her death."

In their reply to the civil suit filed against them, "the Sanborns said they gave Ouellette permission to stay at their home after she told them her parents had kicked her out of their house." The document also stated that the "Sanborns had no duty to call Bob and Lise Ouellette when their daughter appeared at their home that night." Ashley herself "assumed the risk of her injuries or damages." Daniel also denied the allegations against him. The Sanborns then filed for bankruptcy, which stopped the court proceedings; the Ouellette civil case is presently languishing in the court system ("Couple Deny Responsibility in 1999 Death of Teen" 2001).

On May 26, 2001, Robert Ouellette died of a heart attack: he was only forty-nine years old. He saw Ashley's life cut short, but he never did see her killer brought to justice.

Two Cases Cross Paths

In May of 1999—several months after Ashley's death—a teenager in the area had disappeared: and there may be a connection to Ashley's death. Angel "Tony" Torres, who was a likable young man, was attending Framingham State College in Massachusetts. His father, Narciso, said, "He was a good son who always made time for his family. His last trip home was no different. He came to honor his mom on Mother's Day, and it was just like any other visit. Telling us how he was doing at school, and life seemed good for him."

Tony was fond of his former high school friends, and he always got together with them when he came home. Everyone was still talking about Ashley's death after the spring break from college. One night when Tony was home visiting his parents, he made a startling comment about Ashley's murder.

Narciso said:

> We were in the living room watching the news and the story of Ashley Ouellette came up and he immediately said, I know who killed her. I knew the people who killed her. He didn't tell us who but he said he knew who did it, and he said it in such a way that he left no doubt. And I cautioned him. You're either going to the police with this information or you're going to keep your mouth shut, but be careful who you share this with.
>
> At the time I didn't know how much to believe that he actually knew and the little bit of, a little part of me feared for him. Because, you know, witnesses can be silenced. I wish I could go back now and pick him up by his shirt and say "We're going to the police right now." But I didn't do that. (CRIMEWATCH 2016)

Angel "Tony" Torres

Tony's parents went on to say that one night their son went to a party at his ex-girlfriend's residence. Jay Carny, who was a good friend of the Sanborns, was also there. For some reason Tony and Jay went off to a store, which was only a short distance away. Shortly afterward, Jay returned alone. When he was asked about Tony, he said that someone in a red pickup truck picked him up at the store. Tony, however, went missing—never to be seen again.

While Tony had been declared dead since 2004, his body has never been found. Did Tony get involved with the wrong crowd? Were they suspicious that he might start talking too much? There is also some suspicion that drugs might have been involved. It is of interest to note that Jay eventually died of a drug overdose. Tony's family and others suspect that his disappearance is somehow connected to Ashley's murder. What do you think?

Killer Still Remains Free

After seventeen years of countless interviews, detailed searches of the Sanborn residence, a thoroughgoing search of Daniel's car, fingerprinting various people, and carefully reviewing Ashley's last hours, the authorities were only certain that someone had strangled Ashley. And as the months turned to years, there were still no arrests.

From the very beginning, it appeared that information might be forthcoming on the results from any DNA testing that might have been done, but nothing has been revealed. In April 2015, *The Current: Covering Scarborough, Cape Elizabeth and South Portland* reporter Kate Irish Collins said, "The state police are not sharing, as far as I know, any results of DNA testing" regarding the Ashley murder.

In the intervening period of time, the police learned much more about Daniel. "He has been in and out of prison and jail for charges ranging from drugs, theft, and even weapons charges but he has never been charged with anything regarding Ashley" ("Ashley Erin Ouellette—Her Killer Remains Free" 2015a).

What Do You Think?

We'll discuss three possibilities and start with the least likely one.

It's conceivable that sometime after Ashley chose to stay at the Sanborn home she changed her mind again. And for some reason, in the very early hours of Wednesday morning, she decided to leave quietly.

It was the middle of winter, and most likely she started hitchhiking a ride right away. It isn't likely she got very far before a male motorist stopped and offered her a ride. In any event, she met up with the wrong person. Ashley was vulnerable and no match for her assailant, who ended up strangling her and left her lying in the middle of the road.

While we think this scenario is within the realm of possibility, it is not likely at all.

Steven

Ashley's mother said that she did not know why her daughter decided to go to the Sanborn residence or how she even managed to get there. We think it's likely that she wanted to see Steven, who was her former boyfriend. And as we learned, Steven told the police that he had a brief sexual relationship with Ashley several years ago.

There was no story line of evidence that pointed to Steven. And his interview with the police did not appear to be inconsistent. The question of his guilt or innocence, however, remains open. But if he wasn't guilty, was he an accessory to the crime?

Daniel—Try and Catch Me

The pointed line of evidence that the police had accumulated against Daniel led them to think that he was a strong suspect in Ashley's murder. Furthermore, his responses in the interviews were inconsistent.

While the detectives felt they had a good idea of what had happened from the time Ashley was last seen at the Sanborn home to when she was found in the roadway, they did not release any details. But, they did not have a conclusive case—there was no motive and no confession. And no one was speaking out.

Crime Watch Daily confirmed that Daniel had a long rap sheet. And that "he's been convicted of assault on a police officer and spent three years in prison, after being busted for heroin possession with intent to distribute."

If, however, Daniel were guilty, then how would the other members of his family feel with that burden of guilt? Or if he were innocent—how would he and his family feel knowing that the police and many in the community probably felt otherwise?

The overwhelming evidence, however, points to Daniel as Ashley's slayer—and we think he is guilty. We also think that it's more likely than not that the disappearance of Tony Torres was related to what he knew and how outspoken he might have been to the wrong people. What do you think? Who was responsible for Ashley's murder? And where is her killer?

Aftermath: The Truth Is Out There

Friends of Tony Torres stated that the last time they saw him was on May 21, 1999, around 2:00 a.m. in the Sacco-Biddeford area in Maine. His friends maintained they dropped him off and that he was looking for a ride to North Conway, New Hampshire. Tony's parents then notified the police that he was missing when he did not show up for work on May 24, 1999.

If you have any information regarding either Ashley Ouellette or Angel "Tony" Torres, please call the anonymous tip line 201-620-8009. ("Ashley Erin Ouellette—Her Killer Remains Free" 2015b)

In February 2016, the Scarborough police have appealed for information from anyone concerning the death of Ashley Ouellette. Their online appeal in part read:

> "No one deserves to have their life end in this way, especially not a 15-year-old child," the police department wrote. "Seventeen years of waiting for people who have been hiding information to finally come forward. Now is the time."
>
> "If you have any information that you have held back in sharing for any reason, please reach out today. We need those missing puzzle pieces to finally bring justice to the Ouellette family."
>
> Anyone with information about the girl's death should contact Detective Don Blatchford at 730-4312. ("Scarborough Police Appeal for Information in Cold-Case Killing of Ashley Ouellette" 2016)

She Left No Trace

It was December 7, 1939—a cold wintry night—when author Barbara Newhall Follett, who was a child prodigy novelist, walked away from her apartment—never to return or to be seen again. Earlier that evening, she had quarreled with her husband, Nickerson Rogers, over their serious marital problem concerning his infidelity. Barbara not only was angry and depressed when she left their apartment but had very little money. One doesn't just disappear—but she did. Where did Barbara go? And what happened to her?

At the time, the country was still going through a ten-year-long Great Depression. Arguably, it was the darkest economic time in American history. Many people were on the move seeking a better life anywhere: it was "hard times" everywhere.

Curiously, her husband, Nick, did not notify the authorities until two weeks after she left. And it took him four months later to finally request a missing-persons bulletin. Incredibly, no one made any serious attempt to find out what happened to her.

There was no evidence to indicate that foul play might have been involved in her disappearance. Furthermore, her body was never found, and the circumstances and date of her presumed death are utterly unknown.

It's of interest to note that her writing was often about escape when she wrote about her early childhood. The final words in her first novel, *The House Without Windows*, which she had written when she was only twelve years old, described a young girl named Eepersip, who disappears into the woods forever.

"She would be invisible forever to all mortals, save those few who have minds to believe, eyes to see," Follett wrote. "To these she is ever present, the spirit of Nature—a sprite of the meadow, a naiad of lakes, a nymph of the woods" (Collins 2011).

Barbara, too, vanished in the blink of an eye, and over eight decades later, her disappearance still mystifies us.

Early Childhood

Barbara Newhall Follett was born in Hanover, New Hampshire, on March 4, 1914. At the time, her father, Roy Wilson Follett, was an English professor at Dartmouth College. Follett was also a critic and an editor, and his wife, Helen, was a writer.

Roy Wilson Follett and daughter Barbara

Barbara's parents decided to homeschool her because they felt she could learn much better at her own pace. She was interested in words and letters even at the age of three. When she was four years old, she became fascinated with her father's typewriter. One year later, she was using his typewriter to make up words and sentences.

Then she began to correspond with friends and relatives, and before too long she started to write short stories and poems about nature. At age five, she wrote a fairy tale titled, *The Life of the Spinning Wheel, the Rocking-Horse, and the Rabbit.* She didn't have many playmates as a young child, but she had a vivid imagination and had her own animal friends to keep her company—some of which she made up. At age eight, she created a make-believe world called Farksolia with its own language and vocabulary.

In 1927, at age twelve, Barbara published her first book, *The House Without Windows.* It's about a little girl named Eepersip, who lived on top of a mountain, Mount Varcrobis, and was so lonely that she went away to live wild. She talked to the animals and led a sweet, lovely life with them—just the kind of life that I should like to lead. Her parents all tried to catch her, with some friends of theirs, and every time she escaped in some way or other (Stefan 2012a).

The book received high praise from *The New York Times*, the *Saturday Review*, and even from the curmudgeon journalist H. L. Mencken.

Barbara

One year later, in 1928, she published her second book, *The Voyage of Norman D.*, which also received acclaim in leading publications. Her parents then arranged for her to sail as a deckhand with the crew of a three-masted schooner from Connecticut to Nova Scotia that summer. When she returned, she wrote an account of her seafaring adventures as she traveled about on a commercial cargo ship.

In that same year, Barbara's father left her mother for another woman. Barbara, who was fourteen and deeply attached to her father, was stunned and could not believe he would leave his family. It was a turning point in Barbara's life. Just as she reached the pinnacle of her young career, her father, who had always supported and encouraged her, was now abandoning her.

Barbara and her father exchanged letters for a time. She missed him terribly and hoped that he would return home; however, that never

Barbara at age twelve

happened. When she was fourteen years old, Roy wrote to Barbara saying he wanted a divorce from her mother. Barbara, who was heartbroken, began her poignant letter to him with "Dear Daddy:" She ends the letter with "Aren't we ever again going to cross ranges of mountains in all weathers, or play about in Sternway, or steer a real windjammer through the seven seas, or take sailing-lessons from Mr. Rasmussen— as we once planned?" The complete letter can be read on the Internet (Stefan 2012b).

Helen and Barbara

Helen and Barbara were left with little money and had fallen on hard times, and the Great Depression was looming on the horizon. Nonetheless, Barbara talked her mother into taking a voyage to the South Sea Islands and writing about their adventures. They visited Tahiti, Fiji, Samoa, and the Tonga Islands and arrived in Honolulu in the spring of 1929. By the fall, they had returned to California—and they were penniless.

During the voyage, Barbara met twenty-five-year-old E. Anderson, who was a second mate on the schooner *Vigilant*. They spent considerable time together, and according to Stefan, Barbara had fallen in love. When they arrived in California, Barbara became despondent because she missed the wonderful relationship she had with Anderson.

Barbara and Helen then traveled to Pasadena, where they were able to stay with family friends (believed to be the Russell family); Alice Russell and Barbara became close friends, and later they corresponded with each other. Helen was fortunate to have other friends of means who supported her return to Honolulu so she could continue working on the book about their adventurous voyage to the South Sea Islands. Barbara, who was put in care of a guardian, ran off to San Francisco; however, the authorities returned her to her custodian.

Barbara, however, might have returned to Pasadena and also met with Anderson since she said that she wanted to see him. According to Harold McCurdy's book *Barbara: Unconscious Autobiography of a Child Genius*, Barbara had a confrontation with her father and his new wife about her association with Anderson. In any case, Barbara kept up a continuous correspondence with him.

In mid-March, Helen and Barbara were reunited, and they sailed from California to Baltimore, Maryland, where they worked together on their book about their sea adventures (Stefan 2012a).

Shortly afterward, they moved to an apartment in New York City, but they were broke. It was 1930, Wall Street had crashed, and it was the beginning of a decade-long Depression. Barbara, who was sixteen years old, took a course in typing and shorthand. Every morning she rode the subway to her new job as a secretary—one could only wonder what she thought doing that kind of work. She wrote:

My dreams are going through their death flurries. I thought they were all safely buried, but sometimes they stir in their grave, making my heartstrings twinge. I mean no particular dream, you understand, but the whole radiant flock of them together— with their rainbow wings, iridescent, bright, soaring, glorious, sublime. They are dying before the steel javelins and arrows of a world of Time and Money. (Collins 2011)

Barbara Meets Nick

In the summer of 1931, Helen and Barbara rented a cabin in Vermont, where Barbara continued working on her manuscript "Lost Island." That summer she met Nickerson Rogers, her future husband, who was a recent graduate of Dartmouth College and an avid outdoorsman. Barbara and Nick spent the following summer together, traveling the wilderness of New England. While she was still fond of Anderson, her feeling for Nick was becoming more serious, and she decided to stop corresponding with Anderson.

That fall Barbara and Nick sailed to Europe, traveling and hiking in the Alps and the Black Forest. Meanwhile, Helen published her book *Magic Portholes* in 1932, which described their adventures to the South Seas.

In 1933 Barbara and Nick returned to Boston, where he lived, and shortly afterward they got married. Nick worked as an engineer, and Barbara continued her writing. By the mid-1930s, she completed "Lost Island." It was a story about a New York couple who got shipwrecked on a deserted island, but when they were discovered, the woman didn't want to go back to her former life. It remained an unpublished work, because it was difficult to get anything published during the Great Depression. It is now in the public domain and published as *Lost Island: A Romance.*

At around the same time, Barbara finished another manuscript titled "Travels Without a Donkey." It detailed a lively description of the places and experiences of a traveler on the Appalachian Trail—it also was an unpublished work.

Over the next several years in Boston, Nick's job kept him busy so there was little time for hikes into the wilderness and mountains, to Barbara's dismay. While Barbara missed the outdoors, she now became interested in a dance workshop group.

In 1938, she went on a three-week canoe trip with several friends in the wilderness of Canada, which she enjoyed thoroughly. Meanwhile,

Barbara continually kept writing to her friend Alice in Pasadena, telling her all about the things she was doing.

Then in the summer of 1939, Barbara and some of her dance workshop group friends drove across the country to attend a dance workshop in California. She also paid a visit to see her dear friend, Alice, in Pasadena. While visiting Alice, Barbara received a grim letter from Nick, which caused her to return to Boston immediately (Stefan 2012a).

Barbara at age twenty

Barbara Walked Away

Barbara returned to Boston on a Tuesday, but she found their apartment empty. When Nick arrived from New York on Friday, his conversation clearly confirmed that he was involved with another woman. While Barbara was stunned, she did blame herself in part for Nick's behavior; however, she wanted to keep their marriage together. She wrote to Alice explaining that while she and Nick had a serious marital problem, she was hoping that their marriage could be saved.

In early November 1939, Barbara found a new apartment, hoping that a change in living quarters would help keep their marriage intact. At the time, Barbara was working part-time and also dancing part-time. One week later, on December 7, she had a quarrel with Nick about their marriage that apparently could not resolve their difficulty.

One thing led to another, and with only a few dollars in her pocket, she walked out of their apartment. Did she just plan to leave and walk off her anger—not going anywhere in particular—and then return from the cold, wintry night after several hours?

Sadly, Barbara was never seen or no one had ever heard from her again—she was only twenty-five years old. She just vanished.

No One Went Searching

Astonishingly, no one made any serious effort to search for Barbara. Where did she go? And what happened to her? Weeks went by before Nick even went to the police. And he didn't file a missing-person bulletin for another four months. Sadly, it seemed that the world did not care—and in a way, she was forgotten.

About eighteen months later, Wilson Follett wrote an open letter, anonymously, that was published in the May 1941 issue of *The Atlantic*. It was titled "To a Daughter, One Year Lost—from Her father." In part it read:

> This may be the very day when she will come, or word from her or of her, and it seems that the sun is riveted *in situ*, that the hour for the mail stage will never arrive, that the moments are not successive drops in the flow called time, but each a frozen eternity. Yet I am perpetually trying just as hard, just as futilely, to hold back the hours by main strength and so to ward off the moment when the world's news comes in.

Then, some thirteen years later in 1952, Helen apparently found out that Nick did not really look for Barbara. "There is always foul play to be considered," she hinted to Brookline's police chief. To Nickerson, she was blunter: "All of this silence on your part looks as if you had something to hide concerning Barbara's disappearance…You cannot believe that I shall sit idle during my last few years and not make whatever effort I can to find out whether Bar [*sic*] is alive or dead, whether, perhaps, she is in some institution suffering from amnesia or nervous breakdown" (Collins 2011).

According to an article by journalist Paul Collins, the press was unaware that Barbara was missing until 1966, when Helen coauthored a thin academic study on her daughter. Nobody in Boston's morgue matched Barbara, and the bulletin below issued under her married name went unnoticed in the press:

> Brookline. 139 4-22-40 3:38 pm Maccracken. Missing from Brookline since Dec. 7, 1939, Barbara Rogers, married, age 26, 5-7, 125, fair complexion, black eyebrows, brown eyes, dark auburn hair worn in a long bob, left shoulder slightly higher than right. Occasionally wears horn-rimmed glasses.

What Happened to Barbara?

What was Barbara thinking and where was she going when she left their apartment and walked away after learning about Nick's new romance? While she was upset and depressed, was she just getting away to be by herself for a while and then return home to try and talk things over with Nick? But then, she never did return. Was it by choice or did she meet up with foul play? Or was it something else?

There are five possibilities to account for her disappearance that we will discuss: we'll start with the least likely one first.

A New Life

While this possibility is a long shot, it does have a happy ending and so we decided to include it in our story. When Barbara met twenty-five-year-old Anderson on the voyage, she was only fifteen years old. She may have been infatuated with him, and he might have been taking the place of her father. Barbara, however, was mature for her age, and her feeling for him could have been genuine.

As she left her home for the last time that night, did she reflect on how she had been abandoned by her father and then her husband, Nick? Did she then recall that in Anderson's last correspondence he asked her to leave Nick and come to California? Did she somehow find a way to communicate with Anderson and eventually end up joining him in California—and then journey off to a new life in another country?

We do not, however, think her life ended in such a sublime way. But if you are a romantic, it's an attractive option.

Random Killing

When Barbara left her apartment that cold night, she only had thirty dollars and no means of transportation. She was furious and resentful; most likely she wasn't even dressed properly before leaving. She probably just wanted to get away by herself without any particular destination in mind and was not thinking about her surroundings.

She was alone at night and not aware of how vulnerable she was. She may have encountered someone who decided to rob her—women always carry a purse—for whatever money she had.

Perhaps the robbery took an unexpected turn when Barbara angrily fought back. If she began to scream, the mugger may have killed her (even unintentionally) just to keep her quiet. But such a killer would have been very likely to flee the crime scene leaving Barbara behind. Since no body was ever found, we think that this is an unlikely possibility.

Nick—Did He Do It?

When Nick reported Barbara missing, the police not only began to question him but also, because he was her husband, became a person of interest. The authorities became even more suspicious of him when they learned that he did not report her missing for several weeks after she disappeared. Why did it take him four more months to file a missing-person bulletin?

The looming breakup of their marriage did not go over very well with Barbara. While she was bitter and felt betrayed, she thought that her marriage might still be saved. Maybe their quarrel became more serious; however, and tempers flared—then, things quickly got out of hand. Nick lost his temper and in a rage ended up killing her.

He could have wrapped up her body and hauled it out to a Dumpster somewhere in the city where it was never found. There would be no evidence, no body, and no indication of foul play.

While Nick found a new young romance, we think that he had intended to dissolve his marriage legally. He had no motive to murder Barbara, and it would have been stupid for him to go to such extremes—he had other more reasonable options. While he might have been a cad, we do not think he was a killer.

She Chose to Disappear

Even at the age of nine, Barbara wrote a story about a young girl who went out into the woods and vanished into nature. Then at age thirteen, in *The House Without Windows*, she wrote about a lonely child who ran into the wilderness and immediately disappeared altogether. So the themes of escaping and disappearing were reflected in her writings.

We think it is fair to say that she probably fantasized even from early childhood about disappearing into other worlds—both real and imagined. At the time she vanished, the country was still in the latter throes of the Great Depression, and many people were wandering from place to place seeking a better life. And it would have been much easier to disappear then, as many did, than it would be to vanish today.

Was Barbara facing one of those difficult and crucial times in her life, as she left that night—and just wanted to get away from everybody and everything? And was she thinking of how nice it would be to live a new life in obscurity? She might even have continued writing, since she had grown accustomed to writing without publishing.

We believe that she most certainly thought that disappearing might be a solution to her problems, but could she really have cut off forever all contact with everyone who knew her? Maybe, and we think that this is the second-most-likely option. But we think Barbara had something else, something darker in mind—a place where she would never be abandoned again.

Suicide

Barbara had a close relationship with her father, who was very supportive of her writing throughout her childhood: it was a happy time in her life. At age fourteen, however, Barbara was devastated when her father left his family for another woman. As a result, she had very little contact with her father for years. Then in 1937, nine years after her father left, she renewed ties with him, but their relationship was never the same as in those cherished days of childhood.

When Barbara and her boyfriend, Nick, returned from their trip to Europe, they got married, and she seemed to be happy even though she was having difficulty getting her manuscripts published.

But in 1939, when Barbara's marriage seemed to be going well, she was stunned to learn that Nick had a new romance. At first, she was hoping that in some way her marriage might still be kept together—but it wasn't meant to be. Nick just wasn't interested in trying to fix their marital problems.

Barbara was deeply hurt and outraged—she felt as if she was being cast aside yet again. When she left the apartment that night, she probably felt as if no one in the world cared for her. First, her father had abandoned her, and now her husband was leaving.

She most likely felt that there was no way out from the trouble and turmoil in her life—but to escape. We think that she took her own life by jumping from a bridge and was swept out to sea—never to be found. We wonder, what were her final thoughts as she jumped?

In *Lost Island*, she wrote:

You might struggle up a mountainside, tired and aching, thirsty and scratched with brambles, your packstraps cutting into your shoulders as if they were red-hot; but the fight was to a purpose. You would win, stand at last on the crest with triumph. You would unsling your pack and feel light and free as the wind, and go joyfully about the chores of making camp for the night. Stars in the depth of an ice-cold little spring.

Cause of Death: Lynching

"Swinging in the Wind"

The stirring voice of Billie Holiday rings out the words of "Strange Fruit":

> Southern trees bear a strange fruit
> Blood on the leaves and blood at the root.

Those are the first two lines of her famous song protesting American racism. On August 17, 1915—an ordinary day in Georgia—the most notorious and highly publicized murder case in that state ended.

While the defendant claimed throughout the trial that he was innocent, the jury quickly found him guilty of murdering thirteen-year-old little Mary Phagan. The judge sentenced him to death by hanging. While he was sitting alone in jail pondering his fate, the Georgia governor decided to move the prisoner to a more secure state penitentiary for his own protection.

Late one night a band of vigilantes break into the prison and abduct the detainee from his cell: the unruly mob then drive all night to a secluded place to carry out their mission. The leader of the vigilantes takes a piece of rope—an executioner's noose—and places it over the prisoner's head. Minutes later, a dead man's body is swinging from the trees: more strange fruit on southern trees.

His name was Leo Frank. This is the end of the story: a story that starts from a pencil factory in Atlanta Georgia and goes all the way to the US Supreme Court. Leo Frank's story began—and ended—with unspeakable crimes.

Background

Leo Frank was born on April 17, 1884, in Cuero, Texas. When he was three months old, his family moved to Brooklyn, New York. He attended public schools in New York City and in 1902 graduated from Pratt Institute. In 1906 he earned a degree in mechanical engineering from Cornell University; then he worked as an engineer for two different companies.

In 1907, Moses Frank, his uncle, invited Frank to interview for a position with the National Pencil Company in Atlanta, Georgia (Moses was a major shareholder in the company). After accepting the position, Frank traveled to Germany for a nine-month apprenticeship in the manufacturing of pencils. The following year, Frank was promoted to the office of vice-president and then superintendent of the factory. He was only twenty-nine years old.

In 1910, Frank married Lucille Selig of Atlanta, who came from a prominent Jewish family of industrialists. He quickly became a well-known part of the large Jewish community in Atlanta. By 1913, Frank was also serving as president of the Atlanta chapter of B'nai B'rith.

Leo Frank, however, was not popular. It was more that he was a northerner and an industrialist, rather than being Jewish. Atlanta's population had doubled in the past decade, and many new arrivals were seeking jobs in factories and mills. Workers, however, were only earning two-thirds of what northern workers were getting paid. Many of the employees at the pencil factory were teenagers: it wasn't until 1916 that the first federal child-labor laws were written. As a result, there was resentment against northern-owned factories in Atlanta, and newspapers at the time also reflected that attitude.

Leo Frank

Little Mary Phagan: Murdered

Mary Phagan started to work in a textile mill when she was only ten years old. Later, she was employed at the pencil factory, where she operated a machine that placed metal tips on pencils. Mary, who was quite pretty, had deep-blue eyes and an enticing smile. She was four feet and eleven inches in eight and weighed 125 pounds. Mary was a quiet and conscientious worker and attended church regularly. On April 16, 1913, she had been laid off temporarily due to a lack of materials on hand.

Mary Phagan

Around noon on Saturday, April 26, Mary went to the pencil factory to pick up her pay: she had worked twelve hours and earned $1.20. She worked on the second floor of the factory, just down the hall from Leo Frank's office, where she went to receive her wages. She had planned to watch the Confederate Memorial Day Parade with some friends after getting her pay. Mary never met her friends, never saw the parade—and never left the pencil factory alive.

The next day, around 3:30 Sunday morning, Newt Lee, who was the factory security, went down to the basement to use the men's room designated for African Americans. In the drab light of his lantern, which he carried, he was shocked to discover the dead body of a young girl: he then called the police.

Mary had been brutally murdered, and the police were outraged at the condition of her bruised and bloodied body. A strip from her underwear was wrapped around her neck along with a much longer length of rope. The crime scene appeared to show that she had struggled with her killer, and there were indications that she might have been raped.

The police found two crudely written notes—scribbled in pencil—lying on the floor near her body. The notes were written on pages torn from a company notepad of order forms, which they also found nearby. The notes read:

> *mam that negro hire down here did this i went to make water and he push me down that hole a long tall negro black that hoo it wase long sleam tall negro i wright while play with me he said he wood love me land down play like the night witch did it but that long tall black negro did boy his self*

("Leo Frank," *Wikipedia*)

The Investigation

The police proceeded by questioning a number of suspects. Newt Lee told the police that when he found the body he tried to call Frank at his home, but when no one answered, he called the police.

When the authorities attempted to call Frank at his home around 4:00 a.m. that Sunday morning, no one answered the phone. When the police finally contacted Frank at his residence around 7:00 a.m., they sent a patrol car to his house and drove him to the mortuary, where he identified the body. The authorities then took Frank to the factory to view the crime scene.

Later, they drove to the police station, where they asked Frank to examine the two notes found near Mary's body. Frank appeared to be very nervous and requested that his attorneys join him at police headquarters. At the station, Frank pointed out that Lee did not punch his time card every half hour, which he was required to do: indicating that Lee might know more about the murder.

Since the two notes also cast suspicion on Lee, he was arrested and jailed. Meanwhile, one of the detectives arranged to get into Lee's residence and discovered a bloodied shirt at the bottom of a large barrel-shaped container.

Lee then told the police that Frank had requested that he report for work early on Saturday (the day before Lee discovered Mary's body); however, when he showed up at 4:00 p.m., Frank told him to leave and return at his regular time at 6:00 p.m., which seemed odd. Lee said that he then continued on his rounds but did not check the basement until the following day, when he went to use the men's room.

Arthur Mullinax, a former streetcar driver, was also a suspect, since someone reported seeing him with Mary that Saturday night. He knew Mary as a passenger since she often rode the streetcar, which he operated. The police then arrested him on suspicion of being involved in the murder. Both suspects claimed that they were innocent.

By this time, the *Atlanta Constitution* and the *Georgian* were competing fiercely for readers. The *Georgian*, a placid local newspaper purchased by William Randolph Hearst, quickly changed its format using yellow journalism and extra editions to increase its circulation. The hideous rape and murder story was front-page news: the coverage was replete with lurid details and editorials seeking justice.

Suspicion soon also began to develop about Frank's nervous and odd behavior. Detective John Black did not believe that Lee committed the crime all by himself. He felt that someone paid Lee to write those notes, and he began to be more suspicious of Frank.

The Coroner's Jury presented witnesses that suggested Frank was an unethical womanizer. Several former employees stated that he made inappropriate suggestions to woman employees. George Epps, a thirteen-year-old factory worker said that Frank not only flirted with Mary but also frightened her.

Mrs. Nina Formby, a madam in a house of ill repute, said that Frank called her several times on the day of the murder requesting a room for him and a young girl. Formby later recanted her statement suggesting the authorities "plied her with whiskey."

Frank, however, had alibis for the time period that the crime was supposed to have been committed. Nevertheless, the authorities continued to be suspicious about Frank since it took him a week to produce a crucial witness. Lemmie Quinn, who was a supervisor in the area where Mary worked at the factory, stated that Frank appeared to be his normal self that Saturday of the murder. He testified further to Frank's character and said that he felt Frank was not guilty of the crime.

Meanwhile, Frank hired several Pinkerton detectives along with agents from another detective agency to help establish his innocence. Incredibly, in a startling turnabout, they all began working with the authorities and publicly stated that Frank was guilty!

On May 1, Mullinax was released and no longer considered a suspect in the murder. On this same date, less than a week after the murder, the police arrested Jim Conley, an African American janitor at the factory. Conley was seen washing a dirty reddish-stained work shirt at the factory; however, he claimed that he was only trying to rinse out rust stains on the shirt. The police did not test the shirt for blood stains since Conley told them he had been drinking all day Saturday and wasn't near the factory. Witnesses, however, said that they saw Conley loitering around the factory lobby area on Saturday.

The authorities soon learned that Conley had been jailed for armed robbery and served on a chain gang; he also did time on the chain gang for another offense. Furthermore, he was jailed several times for disorderly conduct.

Meanwhile, Solicitor-General Hugh M. Dorsey had convinced the grand jury to indict Frank for murdering Mary: it only took ten minutes to hand down the indictment against him. At the same time, the authorities decided not to take any action against Lee, who was the security at the factory.

On May 5, Mary's body was exhumed since there was some suspicion that she might have been drugged. Dr. H. F. Harris, who examined Mary's body, stated that she had been strangled to death with a cord that was wound around her neck. He said that she had been struck on the head and that there was some facial damage. The doctor also reported that there was evidence of violence on the walls of her vagina, which had been done prior to her death. He said that while she had suffered some sort of sexual violence, he did not find any spermatozoa. Dr. Harris concluded that there was no conclusive evidence of rape or of any drugs in Mary's body.

A second exhumation was carried out on May 6, which was performed to look for fingerprints, which were to be compared with the suspects in the murder. A fingerprint expert was also brought in to assist in the case, but the results were inconclusive.

Conley appeared to be confused when he was being interviewed: he would say one thing and later contradicted himself. At first he said that he couldn't read or write, but further investigation showed that he lied. During the interviews, he continued changing his mind and even admitted lying about the comments he made earlier.

On May 29, two detectives playing good cop/bad cop for three days were satisfied about what Conley had finally told then. The janitor said that Frank had asked him to come to his office since a girl had fallen and hit her head against a machine at the factory; and as a result, the girl had died. Conley said that they both carried the girl's body to the elevator and then descended to the basement, where they dumped the body.

When they returned to the office, Conley said that Frank told him what to write in the two notes and gave him $200, but then he took it back and said he would get the money if everything turned out all right.

Following Conley's statements, Mrs. Magnolia McKnight, the African American cook at the Frank household, told police that Frank's wife, Lucille, told her that her husband confessed to committing the murder. Later, McKnight recanted her statement. Nevertheless, the prosecution felt that they were ready and eager to go to trial. The defense, however, was confident that the evidence against Frank was weak and that he would be found not guilty (Alphin 2014).

The Trial

The trial began on July 20: Hugh M. Dorsey headed up the prosecution team, while Luther Rosser and Reuben Arnold were the two key lawyers for the defense.

The prosecution attempted to show that Frank was guilty based on circumstantial evidence. One expert testified that Mary's blood was found on the floor of a workroom across from Frank's office, but there was no scientific analysis done on the blood. Another expert stated that strands of her hair were found on a piece of machinery in that same workroom, but again, there was no scientific analysis of the hair.

The examining physician stated that Mary was most likely murdered between noon and 12:15 p.m. on Saturday. Dorsey pointed out that Frank said that he was in his office from noon to 12:30 p.m. that day. Since Mary arrived at his office between 12:05 and 12:10 to collect her pay, according to Frank, Dorsey tried to show that Frank was the last person to see Mary and that he had the opportunity to murder her. Monteen Stover, an employee, claimed that she arrived at the office at 12:05 p.m. to collect her wages and left at 12:10 p.m. but did not see Frank, which contradicted Frank's statement as to when he was at the office.

The prosecution team, however, relied mainly on Conley's testimony from his last affidavit during the three-day interview. Dorsey agreed that Conley was seen carrying Mary's body but that he did so only as an accomplice. Conley said that after doing some errands for Frank that Saturday morning, he noticed that when he returned, Frank appeared to be terribly upset and also had a length of rope in his hands. Conley then said that Frank told him that a girl hit her head on a piece of machinery as she attempted to fight off his advances.

Conley then repeated his account of how they took the body down to the basement: later Frank dictated the two notes for him to write and said he would receive money if nothing were said. Conley's coarse and lurid description of Frank's history of sexual behavior with factory girls was so graphic that the judge requested that all women and children leave the courtroom.

Dorsey could not afford to lose this case; otherwise his ambition to seek a higher political office was doomed. Accordingly, he concentrated mainly on Conley's testimony. The last witness for the prosecution was C. Brutus Dalton, a woodworker, who stated that Conley was "on the lookout" while he and Frank met with factory girls in Frank's office as well as in the basement.

Defense Attorney Rosser pointed out that Dalton not only was a convict but also lied when he was cross-examined: we mention this because it becomes important later on. For three days the defense cross-examined Conley, but they were unable to get him to change his story. The defense moved that Conley's comments about Frank's trysts be stricken from the record: the prosecution objected. When the judge ruled to suppress the motion, the courtroom crowd applauded.

A large courtroom was set up to handle the anticipated crowds for the trial. Judge Roan ordered that the windows should be opened because the courtroom was unusually hot. The crowd outside was often loud and unruly, and those inside could hear them shouting, "Hang the Jew," along with other despicable comments; nevertheless the trial went on.

The defense attempted to show that Conley was in error regarding the time Frank was in his office that Saturday. The defense maintained that Mary left the trolley at 12:10 p.m., which was confirmed by the streetcar conductor, and that it took her several minutes to reach the factory. That contradicted Conley's statement regarding the time Mary arrived at the office and also made Stover's comment about Frank not present in his office when she was looking for him between 12:05 and 12:10 p.m. unimportant. Two other employees said they picked up their pay at 11:45 a.m., and not after 1:00 p.m., as Conley alleged. The defense attorneys maintained not only that Conley was seen carrying Mary's body but that he was the primary culprit in the murder.

Frank said that he left the office at 1:00 p.m., and several witnesses testified that they saw Frank leave on his way home between 1:00 and 1:30 p.m. Albert McKnight, the husband of Frank's cook, and also Frank's handyperson both testified that Frank was home at 1:30 p.m., but Conley said he and Frank were in his office at that time.

Frank testified in his own defense: he talked for hours, but there was no cross-examination allowed. He gave an accounting of what he did on the day of the murder and denied any involvement in Mary's murder. He refuted all of Conley's claims and disavowed all the vile stories that the prosecution's witnesses said about his sexual behavior. The newspapers, which were inclined to find Frank guilty, however, viewed his testimony as plausible.

All told, the defense presented about two hundred witnesses, half of who were white and mostly from the north, who testified to Frank's excellent character. Approximately twenty witnesses stated that Conley was a blatant liar.

One of the several office boys who testified for the defense was fourteen-year-old Alonzo Mann, who timidly and nervously affirmed in a soft voice that he never saw C. Brutus Dalton go up to Frank's office with girls or any women going to the superintendent's office. (More about Alonzo Mann later.)

The cross-examination of the defense witnesses focused on Frank's alleged salacious behavior; however, no matter how they replied, Dorsey managed to ask leading questions keeping the sexual implications about Frank alive (Aiuto n.d.).

The Verdict

Since the authorities were concerned that there might be violence if Frank was acquitted, there was agreement that the defense counsel, along with Frank and his family, should not be present in the courtroom when the verdict was announced.

On August 25, 1913, the twenty-fifth and last day of the trial, the jury returned a verdict in less than four hours: they declared Leo Frank guilty. The crowd outside the courtroom yelled, "Hang the Jew."

The next day, Judge Roan sentenced Frank to be hanged for the murder of Mary Phagan, and the execution date was set for October 10. The defense motioned for a new trial, which was set for October 4, assuring at least a delay in carrying out the sentence.

Timeline: Appeals

October 31, 1913—Judge Roan denied a motion for a new trial. Frank's execution date was now scheduled for April 17, 1914.

February 17, 1914—the Georgia Supreme Court also denied a motion for a new trial by a vote of four to two.

February 24, 1914—Conley was sentenced to one year on the chain gang for his part in the murder.

April 6, 1914—the defense attorneys filed a motion to set aside the guilty verdict in the Fulton County Superior Court. The new date for the execution was January 22, 1915.

June 6, 1914—the Fulton County Superior Court denied the motion to set aside the verdict. The defense attorneys then appealed to the Georgia Supreme Court.

October 14, 1914—the Georgia Supreme Court turned down Frank's appeal for a new trial.

November 14, 1914—the Georgia Supreme Court confirmed the trial and judgment in the Frank case.

December 21, 1914—the US District Court rejected the motion to set aside the guilty verdict. The defense attorneys appealed to the US Supreme Court. Frank's execution, which had been set for January 22, 1915, was delayed.

April 9, 1915—by this time, Frank had been in jail for almost two years. The US Supreme Court rejected his last appeal, seven to two. The majority declared that Frank's lawyers waived the right to dispute that the accused had been denied due process since they did not bring up the objection in a timely manner.

US Supreme Court justices Oliver Wendell Holmes and Charles Evans Hughes dissented. Holmes argued, "Mob law does not become due process of law by securing the assent of a terrorized jury." He ended his dissent with the following:

> But supposing the alleged facts to be true, we are of the opinion that if they were before the supreme court, it sanctioned a situation upon which the courts of the United States should act; and if, for any reason, they were not before the supreme court, it is our duty to act upon them now, and to declare lynch law as little valid when practiced by a regularly drawn jury as when administered by one elected by a mob intent on death.

May 31, 1915—the defense attorneys appealed for clemency to the Georgia Prison Commission: the appeal was denied by a two-to-one vote (Georgiainfo.com n.d.).

The Last Chance

The last straw for the defense was to request a commutation of the death sentence to life in prison from Governor John Slaton. Slaton, who was near the end of his term as governor and a leading candidate for the US Senate, followed the Frank case closely.

There was, however, considerable pressure on Slaton by political operatives to deny clemency for Frank; otherwise he would lose their support for his bid for national office. Tom Watson, who had major political power, fed the mob spirit and religious prejudice against Frank. He had served in the US House of Representatives and ran as the vice-presidential candidate with William Jennings Bryan in 1896. He also ran for the presidency in 1904.

The battle lines were drawn: there were supporters on both sides of the issue. Slaton had spent an appreciable amount of time reviewing the case. He even received a letter from Judge Roan encouraging the governor to consider clemency for Frank.

According to author Elaine Marie Alphin, John Boykin (he later became solicitor general) wrote to Slaton: Boykin told him that William Smith, who was Conley's lawyer, said that Conley confessed to murdering Mary. Smith could not reveal what Conley told him because of attorney-client privilege. When Slaton contacted Smith, he would not admit that Conley confessed to him. Smith, however, did present some fingerprint evidence to the governor, which pointed to Conley.

On June 20, 1915, in his last day in office, Slaton did the unpopular thing and commuted Frank's sentence from death to life in prison. He wrote:

> I can endure misconstruction, abuse and condemnation, Slaton said, but I cannot stand the constant companionship of an accusing conscience, which would remind me that I, as governor of Georgia, failed to do what I thought to be right....Feeling as I do about this case I would be a murderer if I allowed this man to hang. It may mean that I must live in obscurity the rest of my days, but I would rather be plowing in a field for the rest of my life than to feel that I had that blood on my hands.

While some newspapers supported Slaton's position, the public was outraged. Solicitor General Dorsey and political operatives railed against the governor in print, and mobs hanged effigies of Slaton and Frank.

The next day Slaton had Frank moved in the middle of the night from the Fulton County Prison to a more secure facility at the Milledgeville State Prison ("Leo Frank," *Wikipedia*).

The Not-So-Safe Haven

On the 17th of July, J. William Green, a fellow inmate, slashed Frank's throat with a butcher's knife shortly after Frank arrived at Milledgeville State Prison. Two other prisoners, who were doctors, managed to stitch the wound and stopped the bleeding. G. D. Compton, the prison doctor, who arrived about fifteen minutes later, said that the quick action of the two doctors saved Frank's life (Alphin 2014).

On August 16, a fleet of automobiles carrying twenty-five men (calling themselves Knights of Mary Phagan) left Marietta, Georgia, and drove about 115 miles to the Milledgeville State Prison. While many lynching mobs are often composed of riffraff, this unruly group of men consisted of some of Marietta's finest citizens: a clergy, a former governor, a US senator's son, a judge, a state legislator, lawyers, an ex-sheriff, a former mayor, and a number of political operatives.

When the lynch party arrived at the prison at night, they cut the telephone lines, overpowered the guards, and handcuffed the warden and superintendent. While some of the men seized Frank, others emptied the gas from the prison's automobiles. The intruders, with Frank in hand, departed swiftly.

They drove all night using back roads; Judge Newt Morris joined them shortly before they arrived at their destination at a grove near Marietta. Frank continued to tell his abductors that he was innocent, but no one was listening: his last request was that they return his wedding ring to his wife. A noose was placed over Frank's head, the hangman's knot was secured around his neck, and then the rope was looped over the sturdy limb of an oak tree.

Around 7:00 a.m., on August 17, Judge Newt Morris restated Judge Roan's statement in court that Frank should be hanged until dead. Author Aiuto wrote that the gathered crowd began shouting, "Hang him hang him, hang the Jew." Then, "fiddling John Carson" started to play and sing "The Ballad of Mary Phagan." The second stanza reads:

> She left her home at eleven
> She kissed her mother good-by;
> Not one time did the poor child think
> That she was going to die.

The Lynching

The Noose

Suddenly the table that Frank had been standing on was swiftly kicked out from under him: Frank was left swinging from the oak tree. When word of the lynching spread, many traveled—including women and children—to the lynching site to see the body. It was a festive event; many took photographs and some even ripped strips of his clothing as well as snipped shreds of rope as souvenirs. Later, these items were sold.

Frank's body was eventually taken to an undertaker in Atlanta, embalmed, and placed on a train to New York: his wife Lucile accompanied him. The private funeral service was held at Mount Carmel Cemetery in Brooklyn (Aiuto n.d.).

Aftermath

November 25, 1915—the Knights of Mary Phagan burned a huge cross on top of Stone Mountain, starting a new order of Ku Klux Klan. Shortly afterward, the American Jewish Committee formed the Anti-Defamation League of B'nai B'rith in New York.

1916—Hugh Dorsey exploited his role in the Leo Frank case and was elected governor of Georgia.

1918—Governor Hugh Dorsey was then reelected as governor.

1920—Tom Watson also capitalized on his notoriety in the Frank case and was elected to the US Senate.

1955—Governor Slaton's action on behalf of Frank led to threats of violence against him. Ironically, he was now assigned protection by the authorities for his own safety. Needless to say, he was also excluded from politics. He and his wife chose to leave the state for a decade before returning to Georgia.

Slaton returned to practice law and became respected in his profession. He then served as president of the Georgia State Bar Association and as a member of the General Council of the American Bar Association. Slaton died on January 11, 1955.

April 23, 1957—Lucille, Frank's widow, never remarried. She did receive, as a grievous moment, her husband's wedding ring. Lucille lived all her life in Atlanta and also worked for years as a salesperson in a women's apparel store. She maintained her husband's innocence to the end. She always signed her name as Mrs. Leo Frank (Georgiainfo.com).

1960s—Following his one-year sentence, Conley spent his life in and out of prison: he disappeared sometime in the 1960s. In 1959, A. L. Henson, an attorney, stated that while Conley was his client, "the man had confessed to him that he had struggled with a girl in the pencil factory but had then blanked out. When Conley came to himself, he was in the basement and the girl was dead. Henson had not spoken out earlier because of lawyer-client privilege" (Alphin 2014).

June 2000—No one in the lynching party was ever arrested or punished; it was decades later before anyone was even publicly identified. Atlanta librarian Stephen Goldfarb posted the list of names on the Internet from research compiled by Mary Phagan's great-niece, Mary Phagan Kean ("Leo Frank," *Wikipedia*).

2004—In his book *And the Dead Shall Rise*, author Steve Oney presents a perceptibly detailed and movingly compelling account of this crime. He does not definitely say who murdered Mary but suggests that Frank was innocent and that it's very likely that Conley was the murderer.

In 1949 William Smith (Conley's lawyer) was in poor health in the Crawford Long Hospital in Atlanta, Georgia. According to author Oney, Attorney William Smith (just before his death) printed out a sentence in block letters and then signed it. The sentence read:

IN ARTICLES OF DEATH, I BELIEVE IN THE INNOCENCE AND GOOD CHARACTER OF LEO M. FRANK

W. M. SMITH

1882–1968—during this period there were 4,773 lynches in the United States. African Americans accounted for 72.7 percent of that number. Mississippi had the largest number, with 581, followed by Georgia, with 531 and Texas, with 493.

The Pardon

March 6, 1982—Alonzo Mann (the fourteen-year-old office boy who testified for the defense) nearly seven decades later signed an affidavit affirming Frank's innocence. Mann admitted that he saw Conley carrying Mary Phagan's lifeless body in the direction that led to the basement that Saturday shortly after the noon hour. He said that Conley threatened to kill him if he told anyone what he had seen.

When Mann told his parents, they told him not to talk about it and not to say anything to anyone. Even after Frank was convicted, he said that his parents continued to tell him to be silent: let sleeping dogs lie.

Mann, now elderly and in failing health, stated that he wanted to tell his story to clear his soul and die in peace. He also passed several lie-detector tests indicating that he was telling the truth.

January 4, 1983—The Anti-Defamation League submitted an application to the Georgia Board of Pardons and Paroles to posthumously pardon Frank.

December 22, 1983—The Georgia Board of Pardons and Parole denied the motion for a pardon stating, while Mann's testimony might implicate Conley, it didn't prove Frank's innocence.

March 19, 1985—Alonzo Mann died: he was eighty-six years old.

March 11, 1986—The Georgia Board of Governors and Paroles announced a posthumous pardon to Frank based on the state of Georgia's inadequacy to protect Frank while he was in custody. The pardon, however, did not exonerate him of the murder.

Guilty or Innocent?

Battle lines were drawn then—and still are today—concerning Conley's guilt versus Frank's guilt. While the timeline for both sides presented witnesses whose comments contradicted each other, we feel that the timeline statements by the defense were much more believable and that the prosecution's timeline statements (based largely on Conley testimony) were not verifiable.

Governor John Slaton, after studying the case closely, commuted Frank's sentence: although he was under great pressure not to do so. It is of interest to note that the judge in the case, Leonard Roan, wrote Slaton urging clemency for Frank.

In 1959, lawyer A. L. Henson, who had been Conley's attorney, stated that Conley eventually confessed to murdering Mary. And John Boykin, who later became solicitor general, wrote Slaton that Conley's defense attorney William Smith told him that Conley confessed to the murder.

Some newspapers at the time and others in the media later felt that Frank did not get a fair trial.

On the other hand, there are those who passionately felt that Frank was guilty then and continue to still feel that way even today. Mary Phagan Kean, the great-niece of Mary Phagan, still believes that Frank was the murderer.

Burning questions, of course, still persist. Why did some of the factory employees lie about Frank? What evidence did the jury have to convict Frank? Was it the court of public opinion, which was prejudiced toward Frank, who was Jewish and from the north, that sealed his fate? And how persuaded was the jury by Solicitor General Hugh Dorsey and the emotional mass hysteria he created? Why did the jury bring in a verdict of guilty in less than just four hours? Was it that citizens of good intent can often turn to violence? Witness the violence of twenty-five citizens, many highly respected in their community, who turned into vigilantes and lynched Leo Frank.

Finally, we believe that Alonzo Mann's signed affidavit late in life asserting Frank's innocence and Conley's guilt is correct. It is not clear if Mann came forward and spoke out at age fourteen, when he had first testified that, it would have made a difference. Nevertheless, in the final analysis, we think that an injustice was done and that Frank was innocent: it was an egregious crime.

This stanza from The Ballad of Mary Phagan suggests that Leo Frank's final judgment may be handled somewhere else.

> Have a notion in my head,
> When Frank he comes to die,
> Stand examination
> In a court-house in the sky.

Mary Phagan

Little Mary Phagan, who was murdered on Saturday, April 26, was laid to rest on Tuesday, April 29, in Marietta in Cobb County, Georgia. A six-foot marble slap lies in front of her gravestone, which reads:

In this day of fading ideals and disappearing landmarks, little Mary Phagan's heroism is an heirloom than which there is nothing more precious among the old red hills of Georgia.

Sleep, little girl; sleep in your humble grave but if the angels are good to you in the realms beyond the trouble sunset and clouded stars, they will let you know that many an aching heart in Georgia beats for you, and many a tear, from eyes unused to weep, has paid you a tribute to sacred for words.

Cause of Death: Firing Squad

A strikingly attractive young girl, Joan Baez, is singing a famous folk ballad at the Woodstock Festival in New York in 1969; Luke Kelly, a hard-living radical Irish folk singer, is also singing that folk song in Ireland; and in 1949, at Paul Robeson's Moscow Concert, he too is singing that same ballad. (At the concert, Robeson makes an audacious decision: he took a surprisingly bold risk that we will tell you at the end of our story.)

Those three performers were all singing "I Dreamed I Saw Joe Hill Last Night." While many know the name Joe Hill and the song, that's about all they know of him. So here is our story about Joe: an ardent labor activist, songwriter, and folk hero.

Joe Hill, like many immigrants, entered the United States in the early twentieth century in search of streets that they heard were paved with gold. As he set off across America, however, he experienced the very difficult conditions of working people, especially migrants. Hill soon dedicated his life to fighting tirelessly in the violent battles between organized labor and industry: his passionate activist manner, however, made him a marked man.

When he was executed for an alleged murder, many came forward claiming that he was railroaded. His controversial death created a legend that transformed a common migrant worker into an American labor martyr.

One of the verses from the song "I dreamed I saw Joe Hill Last Night" by Alfred Hayes, Earl Robinson, which was written after his execution in 1915, keeps his story alive—even to this day.

"The copper bosses killed you, Joe,
They shot you Joe," says I.
"Takes more than guns to kill a man."
Says Joe, "I didn't die."
Says Joe, "I didn't die."

Background

Joe Hill was born as Joel Emmanuel Gävle in Sweden on October 7, 1879. His parents loved music, and they often led the family singing together at home. Hill wrote songs about family members, attended concerts, and played the piano in a local cafe; he also played the accordion, the guitar, and the violin.

His father, Olaf, was a conductor on the railroad. After his father died in 1887, at the age of forty-one, his family faced an economic disaster. Hill, who was only ten years old, had to quit school to help support the family. When his mother died just several years later, the Gävle family of six broke up, and each ventured out on their own. Hill, who did not have an easy life, was disenchanted and began looking for opportunities in some far-off land.

In 1902, at the age of twenty-three, he immigrated to the United States. He worked at various mundane jobs in New York before heading west: moving on to Chicago, where he was employed in a machine shop. Hill, however, was blacklisted for trying to organize the workers at the shop: it was a portent of things to come. He then changed his name from Joel Hagglund to Joe Hill.

In 1905 he spent some time in Cleveland, but he traveled widely, eventually arriving in San Francisco in time for the Great Earthquake in 1906. While he had some knowledge of the English language, which he learned in Sweden, he quickly improved his English doing odd jobs in his travels from New York to California. There isn't, however, much known about what Hill did during his first eight years in the United States.

Here Come the Wobblies

Hill moved to San Pedro, California, in 1910, where he joined the Industrial Workers of the World (IWW), also known as the Wobblies. The origin of the nickname is uncertain; however, we like this most cited theory.

> In Vancouver, in 1911, we had a number of Chinese members, and one restaurant keeper would trust any member for means. He could not pronounce the letter "w" (due to the "I" sounds in the pronunciation of the letter), but called it "wobble" and would ask, "you Eye Wobble Wobble?" and when the red card was shown credit was unlimited. Thereafter the laughing term amongst us was "I Wobbly Wobbly." ("Theory # 1—'Eye Wobble Wobble,'" Industrial Workers of the World—a Union for All Workers)

Hill quickly became active in the organization and served as secretary for the San Pedro local for several years. He soon achieved more status in the IWW organization and traveled a great deal organizing workers for the union. During this period, he wrote many of his most famous songs, including "The Preacher and the Slave," "Casey Jones—the Union Scab," "There Is Power in the Union," "The Tramp," and "Rebel Girl." His songs addressed the experiences of IWW employees from homeless migrants to migrant workers in general. After his Red Songbook was published, the union used his songs in their struggles for higher wages and better working conditions.

Despite his denial, it appears certain that Hill was in Tijuana, Mexico, in 1911 with a group of several hundred Wobblies who attempted to overthrow the Mexican dictatorship of Porfirio Diaz. They sought to seize Baja, California, and free the working class and declare industrial freedom. The takeover lasted only six months: dissension among the ranks, combined with a detachment of trained Mexican troops, forced the rebels back across the border.

Upon his return in 1912, Hill continued to be active, taking part in a protest against the police decision in San Diego to close the downtown section to street meetings. Hill then showed up at a railroad construction workers' strike in British Columbia, where he wrote "Where the Fraser River Flows." It was rumored that he had a secret hideout in the mining town of Rossland in British Columbia. Hill, the radical singer-songwriter, then left Canada and returned to San Pedro, where he provided musical support to the Italian dockworkers who were on strike. In 1913, he was arrested for vagrancy and jailed for thirty days for his overzealous participation in the San Pedro dockworkers' strike. Joe, as you can see, was often seen on the picket line ("Joe Hill," *Wikipedia*).

The Wobblies

What do Helen Keller, Noam Chomsky, and Honus Wagner all have in common? It's a strange combination of names to say the least. The Wobblies, however, had many notable members, including the three we just mentioned. The baseball legend Honus Wagner was rumored (not proven) to be a member; however, the story is so engaging that we wanted to tell it.

The IWW is an international radical labor union, which was formed in Chicago, in 1905. Their goal was to unite all skilled and unskilled workers into one large union for the purpose of overthrowing capitalism and restructuring society on a socialistic basis. They refuted the motto "A fair day's wage for a fair day's work" and inscribed the revolutionary slogan, "Abolition of the wage system," on their banner. The IWW called its philosophy revolutionary industrial unionism. The manner of achieving their goal was through direct action, propaganda, boycott, and strikes. It was opposed to arbitration, collective bargaining, sabotage, and political affiliation and intervention; however, some individuals did advocate sabotage. At its inception, it was the only American union to include women, African Americans, immigrants, and Asians.

The driving force behind the IWW was William D. Haywood, leader of the Western Federation of Miners; Eugene W. Debs of the Socialist Party; and Daniel DeLeon of the Socialist Labor party.

The Wobblies used Hill's songs effectively as a means of social protest and also for organizing workers with varying backgrounds. The protest songs expressed the frustrations and hostilities of the homeless and the dispossessed; from the very beginning, they had a yen for song. Some of their protest songs were "Hallelujah, I'm a Bum" (it was, however, not too popular), "Union Maid," "I Dreamed I Saw Joe Hill Last Night," and the well-known "Solidarity Forever." They even adapted the Salvation Army band song "In the Sweet By and By" to "There'll Be Pie in the Sky When You Die (That's a Lie)."

From 1906 to 1928, IWW carried out 150 strikes involving miners and textile and silk workers. The union reached its peak in 1923, when their membership was estimated to be about 40,000: other sources report slightly higher numbers. The government was able to turn public support against the IWW during World War I since the union was opposed to our participation in the war; as a result, membership in the IWW declined sharply.

By 1930, the union was no longer the influential labor force it once was; however, it does still exist today. In 2005, the centennial of its founding, it had about five thousand members. IWW branches are also located in Australia, Canada, Ireland, Germany, Uganda, and the United Kingdom. ("Industrial Workers of the World," *Wikipedia*).

The Morrison Murders

In the summer of 1913, Hill, who was now a marked man, left San Pedro to visit a sick friend in a hospital in Los Angeles. Afterward, he left for the IWW headquarters in Chicago but stopped in Salt Lake City to earn some money in order to continue on his trip. He found work as a laborer at the Silver King Coalition Mining Company, not far from Salt Lake City. Little did he realize how costly that stopover and temporary job would mean in his life.

It was a frigid Saturday night on January 10, 1914, when John G. Morrison and his two sons, seventeen-year-old Arling and thirteen-year-old Merlin, were getting ready to close their grocery store in Salt Lake City.

Shortly before 10:00 p.m., two armed men masked with red bandannas rushed into the store and shouted, "We've got you now," as they pointed their pistols at John Morrison. They quickly fired several shots, and John immediately fell to the floor. During the holdup, Arling drew a handgun from beneath the counter; however, as he was trying to fire a shot, he was killed instantly. The two killers wasted no time and rushed from the store.

The shooting attracted the attention of John Holt and J. P. Mahan, both of who lived in the vicinity: the two men ran quickly to the store. Merlin, who was now hysterical, called the police: they arrived at the grocery store around 10:15 p.m. By that time, others also were gathered about the storefront. The police immediately took John to the hospital where he died without revealing anything about the intruders.

The Investigation

Holt told the police that he saw two men running from the store and down an alleyway shortly after the shooting. Mahan said that one of the men he saw was bent over and holding his chest as he ran from the crime scene toward the alley.

The police quickly spread out and searched the area thoroughly. The authorities felt they had a fairly good description of the fleeing bandits from Merlin's comments and others who had been in the vicinity of the shooting. At first the police suspected that it was a revenge killing since John Morrison had been a former police officer and might have made some enemies; furthermore, nothing had been stolen. As a result, in the beginning of the investigation several men Morrison had arrested were considered as suspects.

Merlin, however, was not certain in his response to the police whether Arling had shot one of the bandits. Merlin initially said that both killers were about five feet nine inches tall and weighed about 155 pounds. Mahan's daughter said that she also saw one of the men running awkwardly from the crime-scene area as if he had been wounded, shouting, "Hold on Bob. I'm shot." Another woman in the vicinity stated that she heard a man call out, "Oh, Bob."

Frank and Phoebe Seeley told the authorities that they were taking a walk that evening when they met two unpleasant men near the Morrison store shortly before the killings took place. The Seeleys said that they had to step aside since the two scoundrels took over the sidewalk. They went on to say that the taller of the two nasty men was about five feet nine and weighed around 160 pounds. As a result, the police were dealing with conflicting physical descriptions from Merlin and the Seeleys about possible suspects.

The police did not find any of the killer's blood inside the store, and there was no sign of any blood outside at the entrance. Furthermore, the investigators never found any trace of a bullet, which Arling might have fired from his father's .38-caliber revolver. The two murderers entered the store boldly, carried out the killings promptly, and seemed to disappear quickly.

About an hour after the shooting, Peter Rhengreen, a machinist, on his way to work the night shift, came across two men in the general vicinity of the shooting at the store. One of the men was about six feet tall, while the other was somewhat shorter. Rhengreen became uneasy because the taller man began acting peculiar. As Rhengreen quickly walked away, he noticed that the strange man continued to follow him for a while, but then the man finally boarded a streetcar.

Around 11:30 that Saturday night, motorman James R. Usher picked up a shabbily dressed man who was acting rather weird. The man boarded the streetcar through the exit door, stayed on the car, and finally exited near the end of the line.

On that same Saturday night shortly before midnight, Joe Hill knocked on the door of Dr. Frank M. McHugh—just several miles from the scene of the crime—asking to be treated for a gunshot wound in the chest. The doctor quickly assessed the situation and proceeded to attend to Hill's wound. Hill told the doctor that he had been wounded in an argument over a woman. McHugh noticed that Hill's coat did not have a bullet hole but that his other clothing did, indicating he was not wearing his coat when he was shot.

While Dr. McHugh was dressing the wound, Dr. A. A. Bird, a colleague, saw a light in McHugh's office as he was driving by and decided to stop in for a quick visit. After treating Hill's wound, both doctors noticed that he carried a pistol; however, since the gun was in a holster, they only saw the handle. Dr. Bird then agreed to drive Hill to the home of John and Ed Eselius (they were brothers), where Hill was staying at the time. Hill wasn't sure that his pistol was noticed in the doctor's office, but he chose to discard his firearm on the way to the Eselius home. Otto Appelquist, who had previously worked with Hill as a longshoreman, also lodged there.

Dr. McHugh then notified the authorities of Hill's visit and also told them that he carried a pistol. The authorities quickly dropped their revenge theory and focused on Hill.

Sometime around 1:00 a.m. on Sunday morning, as the police were searching the crime scene, a fast-driving taxicab driver pulled up at the storefront and asked the police if they requested a cab. The driver said that a man with a rough voice called and said to quickly hurry to the Morrison grocery store. After the frustrated cab driver sped off, the police picked up the odd streetcar passenger who was now strolling about the area. When they approached him, they noticed that he was quivering badly since he wasn't wearing a coat and it was very cold. He stated that he was just taking a walk and knew nothing about the Morrison murders; furthermore, he said that he had not called a cab.

He told the police that his name was W. J. William, while other accounts said W. Z. Williams. He said he was employed at a restaurant and that he was saying at the Salvation Army: he lied on both counts. When the police searched him more thoroughly, they found that he was carrying a bloody handkerchief. Was the man who called the cab one of the killers who was attempting to help his wounded companion escape?

In his excellent book *The Man Who Never Died*, William M. Adler, wrote, "On Monday morning, the police summoned [motorman] James Usher to the station to examine a rogues' gallery of mug shots. His eyes alighted on one: Magnus Olson, the man Salt Lake City police knew as Frank Z. Wilson. Whether he was still in custody is unclear."

Adler also wrote:

> But this was not the man whom police arrested for murder a day later. That man had no history of crime (save for a vagrancy charge). He did, however, have a fresh gunshot wound, and he looked so much like Frank Z. Wilson that police assumed he was lying when he gave his name as Joseph Hill.

On Tuesday night Dr. McHugh paid a visit to see his patient, Joe Hill; meanwhile, the police told McHugh that they had planned to arrest Hill later that night for murdering John Morrison. Sometime shortly after midnight, Fred Peters and several of his deputies proceeded to arrest Hill: there was an altercation and Peters shot him in the hand.

Shortly after Hill was taken into custody and processed, an editor from the *Herald-Republican* took Merlin, who was the only witness to the crime, to look at Hill in his cell. The next issue of the newspaper headline read, "Wounded Bandit Who Killed Morrisons," and it also stated that Merlin had identified Joe Hill as the culprit who killed his father.

Merlin, however, was indecisive and not that definite about identifying the murderer; nevertheless, the press was reporting that the authorities had declared that the circumstantial evidence all indicated that Hill was guilty. The *Tribune* and the *Herald-Republican* both pointed out "that he [Hill] was gravely wounded, that his accomplice remained at large, and that he was not who he claimed to be." The *Tribune* headline read:

> At an early hour this morning Sergeant Ben Siegfus expressed the belief that Joseph Hill, arrested for the murder of the two Morrisons, is Frank Z. Wilson, a former inmate of the state prison. The description of Hill corresponded closely with that of Wilson. Meanwhile the police had been searching for Wilson ever since the murders. (Adler 2011)

A total of twelve people were arrested before Hill was charged with the murder of John Morrison. The confusion came about because of the striking similarities of the physical features and ethnicities of both Hill and Wilson (whom the police knew as Magnus Olson). They both emigrated from Scandinavian countries: they were in their early thirties, about six feet tall, and weighed around 150 pounds. They had the same light-brown hair, blue eyes, and healthy teeth.

Meanwhile, Otto Appelquist, Hill's alleged accomplice, had disappeared shortly after Hill was taken into custody. Arling's murder, however, was attributed to an unknown accomplice—but it could have been Appelquist. Olson also had fled from the area, but the press and the police were now certain of Hill's guilt.

The Trial

The Prosecution

The trial began on June 17, 1914. District Attorney Elmer O. Leatherwood, who at the time had aspirations for a higher office, began by stating that he would prove that two men—one tall, the other short—were seen close to the Morrison grocery store just before the murders took place and that Hill was the taller of the two men. He said that shortly after the murders, one of the men was seen staggering nearby the store and called, "Oh, Bob, I'm shot" and that he had the physical appearance of the defendant. The district attorney said the state would show that Arling fired a revolver and shot at one of the killers. He went on to say that two doctors would testify that they treated Hill for a gunshot in the chest just several hours after the killings but that he would not tell them the details of how he had been shot. The doctors would also confirm that Hill had been carrying a revolver, which he later discarded. Leatherwood then told the jury that while the state's evidence was only circumstantial, he would provide a series of events that would allow the inference that Hill was guilty. He then called on witnesses who previously gave statements to the police.

Merlin Morrison, the thirteen-year-old son of John Morrison, who was at the store the night of the shootings, was considered to be the state's key witness. Leatherwood started out with a series of leading questions trying to get Merlin to identify the defendant with certainty. Judge Morris L. Ritchie overruled Defense Attorney Ernest D. MacDougall's objection to the leading questions. Merlin, however, was only able to say that Hill had the general appearance of the man who shot his father.

The state chemist then testified that a blood sample he had analyzed, which had been taken from a sidewalk a short distance from the store, was mammalian but could not tell if it was human or not. At that point in the proceedings, Hill suddenly rose to his feet and addressed Judge Ritchie, stating that he wanted to dismiss two of his defense lawyers, Ernest D. MacDougall and Frank B. Scott; however, Ritchie overruled the defendant.

Hill, undaunted, continued to persist that he had a right to discharge his counsel. Ritchie told Hill that if he really meant what he said, then he would go along with his request. Hill's reply was swift: "Yes sir, I mean what I say." Judge Ritchie then told the defense lawyers that they now were amicus curiae (friends of the court) for the remainder of the trial. It soon became clear, however, that Hill was not capable of conducting his own defense, and things went downhill quickly for the defense.

The prosecution managed to find twelve eyewitnesses—none of whom were in the store at the shooting but were in the vicinity—who said that the killer looked like Hill. One witness stated that one of the assailants called out, "Oh Bob" and testified that it sounded exactly like Hill's voice. Another witness stated that she heard one of the men running from the store shouting, "I'm shot" and claimed that the man resembled Hill.

The state then called Phoebe Seeley to the stand, who went over the encounter she and her husband had with the two rude men they met near the Morrison store shortly before the killings took place. Leatherwood—with leading questions—finally got Phoebe to say that the defendant's physical features were very similar to that of the taller of the two men they met on the street that night. Furthermore, she stated that the two men had similar facial scars. Five months earlier, however, when she was asked if the defendant and the crude sidewalk chap were the same person, she replied emphatically that she could not say that. It is of interest to note that Phoebe seemed to be able to recall more details of their encounter with the two men more clearly with the passage of time.

After several days, Attorney Soren X. Christensen, who was an associate of the nationally known criminal and defense labor lawyer Orrin Hilton, now joined the defense team.

Leatherwood tried to show that Arling shot Hill that night with a .38-caliber revolver, which was found close to Arling's dead body at the store. Police detective George Cleveland stated that when he examined the army revolver, five bullets were still in the gun's six chambers and that the weapon smelled like it had been recently fired.

According to author Adler, not only did detective George Cleveland have a shady reputation but an expert witness stated that it was impossible to determine that Morrison's gun had been recently fired since it did not use black powder. Furthermore, a police officer testified that it was common practice to only load five chambers in their revolvers, with the hammer then resting on the empty chamber. John Morrison, who served as a police officer for several years, might have carried over that customary habit into his retired life. But—did he or didn't he?

Leatherwood went on to point out that it was highly suspicious when Hill, who left the Eselius home at around 6:00 p.m., arrived at Dr. McHugh's office with a gunshot wound only about ninety minutes after the Morrisons were murdered. The police found a red bandanna in Hill's room; however, they did not find the pistol that was reported to be in his possession. But why did Hill discard his weapon? Would it have incriminated him?

Dr. McHugh could not tell if the gun shown to him by the state's attorneys resembled the pistol that Hill had on him that night in his office. McHugh said that he was not sure what kind of gun was used to shoot Hill but that it was larger than a .32-caliber revolver: Dr. Bird insisted that Hill's gun was a .38-caliber Colt, which the prosecution showed him—the same type of gun that was used to murder the Morrisons.

The district attorney pointed out that Hill's refusal to testify was evidence that he was guilty. (At the time they were not violating Hill's rights under the Fifth Amendment; it would be, however, grounds for reversal today.)

Leatherwood concluded his remarks by pointing out that Hill's refusal to (a) name the woman who was involved in the argument that got him shot, (b) fully explain the circumstances of his wound, and (c) identify those who were involved in shooting him suggested that Hill knew his story could not be corroborated. Leatherwood also pointed out that it was strange that the woman involved did not come forward to save Hill.

On June 22, the prosecution rested its case. The defense team moved to dismiss the case on the basis that there was no credible evidence of Hill's guilt. Judge Ritchie denied the motion.

The Defense

The defense team of Ernest D. MacDougall, Frank B Scott, and Soren X. Christensen called a total of eleven witnesses.

Mrs. Betty Eselius Olsen, who was a sister to the Eselius family and served as their housekeeper, was the first witness for the defense. She testified that she had given Hill a red bandanna the day after he was wounded and that there were other such handkerchiefs in the household for the Eselius men who lived there.

Merlin admitted in cross-examination that the killers wore bandanna handkerchiefs that covered their faces except for their eyes and that they also wore hats. As a result, he was unable to positively identify Hill as the murderer. Understandably, there were also some inconsistencies from thirteen-year-old Merlin regarding the physical description of the two men who committed the murders. The prosecution also failed to get a positive identification from Phoebe that the man she saw that night was Hill. The defense pointed out that many others also matched the dubious description of the murderer.

The defense chose to treat Merlin with kid gloves. He was a youngster after all, and they were concerned that he might break down: they wanted to avoid that from happening, which would most likely have influenced the jury. Hill, however, was annoyed and waned his attorneys to question Merlin rigorously.

Hill's attorneys pointed out that he did not know Morrison, and since there was no robbery, he did not have a motive to kill him. Hill's lawyers then alluded to the fact that Morrison always feared reprisals from men he had arrested and that his death was a revenge killing. He told his wife; John Hemple, a former police captain that he worked for; as well as Herbert Steele, a neighbor, that he felt his life was in danger.

The defense also pointed out that one of the murderers cried out, "We've got you now." Furthermore, there were two earlier attacks on Morrison's life—one in 1903 and another in 1913, indicating that someone had a motive to kill him—suggesting that Hill did not have a motive, but someone else did.

When motorman Usher testified at the trial, he said that Frank Z. Wilson—an alias that Magnus Olson used—"sat hunched over in his seat all the way to town." Usher also stated that his passenger did not resemble Hill.

The defense pointed out that the man, identified as W. J. Williams or W. Z. Williams walking around near the grocery store shortly after the shooting, had a bloody handkerchief in his pocket. Was he one of the killers, looking for his companion? Williams also lied to the police when he was asked where he lived and what he did. The man's only comment was that he was innocent: the police eventually released him. Williams was most likely Wilson—an alias, which Olson used.

The defense showed that the bullet hole in Hill's jacket did not match with the wound in his chest: the hole in his jacket was about four inches lower than the exit wound in his back. But, when Hill raised his hands overhead as he did when he was shot, the bullet hole in the jacket matched with the wound to his chest. Dr. M. F. Beer, a surgeon, who had examined Hill prior to the trial, when called to testify, agreed to the defense's description.

Scott then asked Dr. Beer if it was possible for the bullet to have hit Hill with his arms in any other position than raised overhead. Leatherwood immediately objected: Judge Ritchie, as usual, sustained the objection. Scott, however, made his point. The *Herald-Republican* reported that Dr. Beer believed that Hill was shot while he was holding his hands overhead. Furthermore, the bullet that went clear through Hill's body was not found in the store at the crime scene, nor was any of his blood.

Dr. Beer also stated that Hill's exit gunshot wound was incompatible with a lead bullet. A lead bullet leaves a ragged wound several times larger than the entrance wound. The bullet that entered Hill's chest left only a slightly larger exit wound. Hill, therefore, had been struck with a steel bullet, which was not manufactured for John Morrison's .38-caliber revolver.

Hill, however, maintained that his gun was a Luger .30, which he bought at the local pawnshop. While the record in the store showed that Hill had purchased a gun on December 6, 1913, there was no indication of the make or caliber gun; and the sales clerk was in another city at the time the authorities visited the store. When Hill's lawyers contacted the sales clerk, he said that he remembered selling a Luger at that time.

The defense pointed out that there was no evidence to directly connect Hill with the murder. Furthermore, Merlin, the prosecution's key witness, was unable to present any concrete testimony against Hill. The defense felt that they managed to show that Wilson could certainly have been implicated in the crime, which would cast a shadow of reasonable doubt regarding the guilt of Hill. There were no more witnesses to take the stand: the question remained—would Hill testify?

Hill's attorneys were divided regarding whether Hill should take the stand. MacDougall and Scott were in favor of Hill taking the stand, but Christensen opposed. Counsel for the defense then asked for a brief recess to discuss in private what they should do. The defense chose to rest.

Hill chose not to testify at the trial because he believed he did not have to prove his innocence; furthermore, he believed that the prosecution could not prove him guilty. Hill, however, steadfastly denied killing Morrison.

On January 27, 1914, the case went to the jury. They took only six hours and forty minutes to decide the case. The brief trial was due, in part, to Judge Ritchie's rulings to suppress important witnesses along with restricting their testimony. Hill listened to the reading of the verdict indifferently: there wasn't any change in color in his face. The police were expecting a demonstration by the IWW supporters, but there was no disturbance. On Saturday, June 28, 1914, at 10:00 a.m., the court clerk read the verdict: Joe Hill was guilty as charged ("Joe Hill," *Murderpedia*).

Olson and his partner, Thomas Waite, were picked up several weeks after the Morrison murders on a robbery charge. Olson only spent about two years in prison of his ten-to-eleven-year sentence. Magnus Olson (alias Frank Z. Wilson) was then paroled. Waite, as a first-time offender, spent about one year in prison of a fourteen-to-sixteen-month sentence. He was released from prison in March 1915. Waite's prison file revealed that he weighed 156 pounds and stood five feet eight and a half inches in height. It is of interest to note that Merlin's early description of one of the murder suspects was that he was about five feet nine tall and weighed about 155 pounds. Phoebe, however, stated that the taller of the two discourteous men she and her husband had encountered prior to the killings had a scar-like mark on the side of his face. Waite's prison record showed that he had a scar on his right cheek (Adler 2011).

The Execution

On July 8, Judge Morris L. Ritchie gave Hill the option to be hanged or shot. Hill said, "I'll take shooting. I'm used to that. I have been shot a few times in the past and I guess I can stand it again." Ritchie set the execution date for September 4; however, he then granted a stay pending a new trial. On September 1, 1914, Judge Ritchie denied the petition for a new trial.

Hill spent the next twenty-two months in prison while his case went through the appeals process. Thousands of letters and many petitions became part of the campaign to save him. In the spring of 1915, the defense brought in a well-known criminal defense and labor lawyer named Orrin H. Hilton. Hilton appealed his case to the Utah Supreme Court; however, after hearing the case the court said there was no cause to grant a new trial or to reverse the jury's verdict: the decision was handed down on July 3. Later, Hilton was disbarred by the state of Utah after he gave a speech at Hill's funeral. On August 2, 1915, Judge Ritchie sentenced Hill to die: the execution was set for October 1, 1915.

William D. Haywood urged Hill to take his case to the US Supreme Court. Hill said not to waste the money; but it turned out that his supporters lacked the funds to appeal his case to the higher court. Chief Justice Edward Douglas White's US Supreme Court, however, showed its conservative nature in the Leo Frank case (our previous story in the book), so it may not have done much good anyway. At the time, Judge James Clark McReynolds, who was a recent appointee, further strengthened the conservative composition of the high court. Furthermore, Hilton also felt that there was no reason to believe that the US Supreme Court would intervene.

Hill's attorneys now appealed to the Utah Board of Pardons for a commutation of the sentence to life imprisonment. Hilton requested that the Utah Board treat Hill similar to the way the governor of Georgia had intended to do for Leo Frank: commute his sentence pending further investigation of the case. The board, however, denied the appeal on behalf of Hill. On October 18, Hill was now sentenced to die for the third time: Judge Ritchie set the execution date for November 19, 1915.

The Swedish ambassador to the United States sent President Woodrow Wilson a telegram seeking clemency for Hill. On September 30, 1915, President Wilson wrote William Spry, governor of Utah, requesting that Hill's execution be delayed, pending a full investigation: it turned into a major media event. Nevertheless, Governor Spry would not pardon Hill. People around the world also tried to save him. It was the end of the line: eventually, no one could save Joe Hill.

When Hill heard the bad news, he sent a farewell message to IWW leader Bill Haywood. He wrote: "Goodbye Bill. I die like a true rebel. Don't waste any time mourning—organize! It is a hundred miles from here to Wyoming. Could you arrange to have my body hauled to the state line to be buried? I don't want to be found dead in Utah."

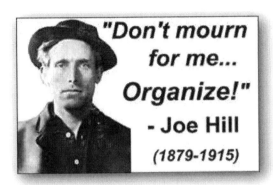

The day before his execution, a prison guard stated that around 10:00 p.m., Hill handed him a piece of paper: it was his last will.

My Last Will

My will is easy to decide
For there is nothing to divide
My kin don't need to fuss and moan
"Moss does not cling to a rolling stone."
My body?—Oh!—If I could choose
I would to ashes it reduce
And let the merry breezes blow
My dust to where some flowers grow.
Perhaps some fading flower then
Would come to life and bloom again
This is my Last and Final Will.
Good luck to all of you.

Joe Hill

Hill awoke around 5:00 a.m. on Friday, November 19, 1915: it was D-Day for Joe. After several hours, he was taken from his prison cell out into the prison yard. The five-man firing squad was hidden in a blacksmith's shop, which was draped over with canvas with five holes: one hole for each of five rifles aimed at Hill twenty feet away. All rifles were loaded, but one contained a blank cartridge. The blank was issued out randomly to one of the shooters so that no one individual would know who fired the live round, which is referred to as the "conscience round."

Hill was sitting on a chair: a mask was placed over his eyes and a small paper target was pinned to his chest directly over his heart. Hill called out, "I am going now boys. Good-by." And again he cried out, "Good-by Boys." The firing squad leader shouted, "Ready, aim," but then Hill quickly shouted, "Fire—go on and fire." Then, the final command from the firing squad leader to fire: it was all over.

Shortly before 8:00 a.m., three bullets hit the small target over his heart—Joe Hill was pronounced dead (Smith 1969).

In his final hours, Joe Hill probably said it best of all: "I have lived like a rebel and I shall die like a rebel."

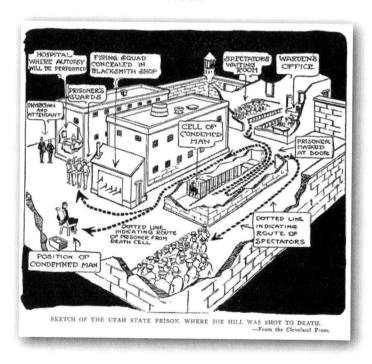

SKETCH OF THE UTAH STATE PRISON, WHERE JOE HILL WAS SHOT TO DEATH.
—From the Cleveland Press.

Did He or Didn't He?

What we know is that Joe Hill, on the night that John Morrison and his son Arling were murdered, visited Dr. Frank McHugh's office just several miles from the crime scene to be treated for a gunshot wound. We also know that the authorities did not find any evidence of the killer's blood at the crime scene. In addition, the police were unable to find any lead bullet fired from Arling's gun. It is unclear whether Arling ever fired his father's gun or that he shot anyone.

Both doctors stated that Hill had a pistol in a holster while he was being treated for his wound. Shortly afterward, Hill said that he discarded the gun so he was unable to prove that his Luger was not the murder weapon.

Several witnesses for the state testified that one of the men running from the store resembled Hill; however, since the two killers were masked in red bandannas, they relied on the overall physical appearance of the killer and not his facial features. A witness said that one of the killers shouted, "Oh, Bob." Later, she said that he sounded exactly like Hill when she heard Hill speak. At first, thirteen-year-old Merlin Morrison, who was an eyewitness at the crime scene, told the authorities that he was unable to identify Hill, but then later he changed his mind to say that one of the killers did look like Hill.

The prosecution maintained that Hill's refusal to explain the circumstances of his shooting as well as his defiance not to testify at the trial pointed to his guilt. District Attorney E. O. Leatherwood, by his own admission, told the jury that while his case was based on circumstantial evidence, it was detailed, convincing, and sufficient to get a conviction.

On the other hand, was Hill arrested mainly on suspicion, having the misfortune of getting shot on the same night that the two Morrison men were murdered? Ordinarily, the conditions of his arrest—with no concrete evidence—would have most likely resulted in his release. But was it the case that when the authorities realized that Hill was the suspect and knowing that he was a member of the IWW and also a radical union agitator that the anti-Wobbly element in Utah moved forward to convict him?

Some felt that Hill's refusal to provide information on his injury and the woman and his rival who allegedly were involved was a pivotal mistake and going too far to protect somebody. But why didn't Hilda or Appelquist speak out to save Hill? If Hilda's two rivals were feuding over her at the time of the murder, who killed the Morrisons? Or was it possible that in his own mind, he wanted to be a martyr for the cause he so deeply believed in? There has been, however, speculation on this issue for over a century.

Yet more than five decades later, it is haunting to think that an innocent man was put to death. Is it possible that Hill was innocent and had been framed by the authorities in Utah? While the state of Utah was unable to prove that Hill was involved in murdering the two Morrison men, he might have been guilty of sin.

In 1946, Dr. McHugh made public an alleged confession by Hill to murdering the Morrisons in an interview with Vernon Jensen, who became interested in the case. According to author Gibbs M. Smith, Jensen said that when McHugh visited Hill at the Eselius home several days after treating him for his wound, Hill then spoke out saying:

> I'm not such a bad fellow as you think. I shot in self-defense. The older man reached for the gun and I shot him and the younger boy grabbed the gun and shot me and I shot him to save my own life. He also added, I wanted some money to get out of town.

Jensen said, "As a socialist and disbeliever in capital punishment he did not want to see Hill executed. Since he was never asked if he received any other explanation of Hill's wound, McHugh chose not to tell all he knew." The Jensen interview is the sole source of the alleged confession by Hill. Author Smith said that when he interviewed Mrs. McHugh she did not have any knowledge of the confession. While there is no way to confirm the thirty-year-old McHugh story, we believe that Hilda Erickson's letter is more credible than McHugh's interview with Jensen.

In 2011, author William M. Adler's well-researched book *The Man Who Never Died* reveals new information that was not introduced at the trial. Adler wrote that Hill and his friend, Otto Appelquist, were competing for the affection of twenty-year-old Hilda Erickson, who was related to the Eselius family. Adler found a letter from Hill's girlfriend, Hilda, which confirmed that she was engaged to Appelquist but that she broke the engagement. She also affirmed her relationship with both Hill and Appelquist and the competition between the two men. The letter indicated that Appelquist had shot Hill that night out of jealousy. Hilda maintained that she never heard from Appelquist when he left shortly after the murders. Adler also suggested that Hill did not testify in part because he wanted to protect Ms. Erickson's privacy. He said that Ms. Erickson wrote the letter in 1949 to Aubrey Hann, who was planning to write a book on Hill, but he never finished it. Adler maintains he found the letter in papers, which were stored in Hann's attic.

In researching Magnus Olson's background for about a year, Adler learned that Olson (alias Frank Z. Wilson) had used numerous aliases in his checkered criminal past and that he was on a crime binge in the area for about six weeks before the night the Morrisons were murdered. In 1911, Olson had also spent time in prison in Utah. According to Adler, the evidence against Olson—as Wilson or Williams—whom the police originally suspected of the Morrison murders, was more convincing than the case made against Hill (Adler 2011).

Since the prosecution was unable to conclusively establish Hill's guilt, we feel that he should not have been executed. But if we ask the question, Did he or didn't he? we are led to think that it is more likely that he did not commit the crime. If Joe Hill did not commit the crime, then who murdered the Morrisons? The circumstantial evidence points to Magnus Olson—alias Frank Z. Wilson—as a more likely suspect.

While this aspect of Hill's life—guilty or innocent—tends to fade, his legend as a labor activist and Wobbly songwriter still lives on.

Aftermath

Joe Hill became more famous in death than he was in life. Even one hundred years after his death, his status as a labor icon and the controversy about his conviction have not died.

His body was sent to Chicago, where it was cremated. His ashes were supposedly placed in hundreds of small envelopes and sent to IWW locals in every state but one (no surprise), as well as supporters in countries around the world. The envelopes were to be opened on a specific date; however, there was some delay in all the envelopes reaching their destination. Nevertheless, Hill's ashes were eventually scattered to the winds around the globe. It was a way to get Joe back among his own kind of people again.

Hill was immortalized in song and poetry, including the widely known ballad "I Dreamed I Saw Joe Hill Last Night," which was adapted by Joan Baez, Pete Seeger, Paul Robeson, and others. It is of interest to note that Hill is best remembered for a stirring song he did not write.

In the very beginning of this story, we said that we would tell you more about Paul Robeson. When Robeson performed at the Moscow Concert in 1949, he publicly stated that he had seen Isaac Feffer, one of the many who disappeared under Stalin's reign; the audience gasped. And when Robeson started to sing the song of the Warsaw Ghetto, "We will survive, we will survive," there was a mixture of cheers and boos from the audience. His voice crackled with passion and rage. His bold public brave defiance of Stalin was immensely courageous. In 1950, Robeson was blackballed and stripped of his passport by the United States. And in 1952, Isaac Feffer, a soviet Yiddish poet, was executed at Lubyanka prison.

Over the years, there were countless acknowledgments paid to the famous wobbly protest singer: poems were written in his honor; songs eulogized him; biographies extolled Hill, and one was made into a movie; several books were published on his life; musical tributes were created to praise him; and even a postage stamp in Sweden was issued in his honor.

The songs that Hill wrote were also sung by numerous folksingers around the world, including Billy Bragg, Ami DiFranco, Bob Dylan, Woody Guthrie, Utah Phillips, Bruce Springsteen, and many others.

In 2004, Utah stopped offering inmates their choice of death by a firing squad. Ronnie Lee Gardner, however, was one of several prisoners on death row who was sentenced before the law was changed and therefore still had the option of facing a shooting party. In 2010, he was the last inmate to be executed by a firing squad in the state of Utah ("Utah Lawmakers Vote to Become Only State to Allow Firing Squad" 2015).

On March 10, 2015, the Utah Senate approved legislation that would allow the use of a firing squad to carry out the death penalty if injection drugs are unavailable. In the spring of 1915, Utah governor Gary Herbert signed the bill bringing back the firing squad as a method of execution.

Lincoln Caplan wrote:

> Since the report [American Law Institute—2009], six states have abolished the death penalty, most recently Delaware in the summer of 2016, bringing to 20 the number of states that do not have it. Of the 30 that do, 14 are not carrying out executions because of a formal or an informal moratorium. Only 17 states have executed any death-row inmates in this period—including Delaware, before it abolished the punishment. Just six states have executed more than 70 percent of those inmates. One of those states, Oklahoma, now has a formal hold on executions during an investigation of its method of lethal injection. The death penalty is in flux in most of the states that still have it on the books. (Caplan 2016)

Executions in the United States are at a twenty-five-year low—and the downward trend appears to be continuing. Joe Palazzolo wrote: "Roughly 1,900 inmates were on death row in July 2016, down from a peak of about 3,500 in the first decade of the twenty-first century, according to the Bureau of Justice Statistics and the NAACP Legal Defense and Education fund."

Palazzolo also pointed out that "A combination of forces—a dwindling supply of lethal drugs, a key US Supreme Court decision and growing scrutiny of expert testimony and evidence—have contributed to the slowdown in executions, legal experts said" (Palazzolo 2016).

The Big Boston Heist

In the wee hours of Sunday morning on March 18, 1990, two men disguised as Boston police officers carry out one of the most infamous art thefts in history. After parking their red hatchback close to the Isabella Gardner Museum in Boston, they wait patiently until the streets are deserted. The two men then leave their vehicle and walk deliberately up to the side entrance of the museum—it is 1:24 a.m.

After one of the fake police officers presses the buzzer, they gain entrance by posing as police officers responding to a call. Once inside, they apprehend the two security guards under the guise of arresting them. After handcuffing the guards, they lead them down a stairway where the intruders secure the guards to fixtures in the basement.

In just eighty-one minutes, the thieves roam through the galleries and manage to steal thirteen works of art valued at over $500 million. Their thievery earns them a whopping $6.2 million per minute! They make off with a fabulous collection that included art by Rembrandt, Vermeer, Manet, and Degas and a bronze Chines goblet that dates back to 1200 BCE: it was the largest property crime in US history. While it was an audacious feat, it was also a barbaric act.

Even after twenty-six years, despite thousands of tips and leads including a $5 million reward for the recovery of the art, none of the artwork has ever been returned.

Background

After Isabella Stewart Gardner received a large inheritance from her father in 1891, she started collecting art seriously. Gardner continued collecting art throughout her married life and also sought out experts to assist her in acquiring major acquisitions. In 1898, when her husband, John L. Gardner, died, she began planning a shared dream they had of building a museum for their prized art treasures.

In 1903, the Isabella Stewart Gardner Museum was finally completed in the marshy Fenway area of Boston. The magnificent four-story museum was constructed in the style of a thirteenth-century Venetian palace with a stunning courtyard.

The museum houses a world-class collection of more than twenty-five hundred pieces of American, European, and Asian art. Botticelli, Degas, Manet, Michelangelo, Raphael, Rembrandt, Sargent, Vermeer, and Whistler are some of the artists represented in the galleries. In addition to the rare paintings, the museum also displays sculpture, drawings, ceramics, textiles, illustrated manuscripts, and rare books.

When she died in 1924, Gardner's will provided for an endowment of $1 million ($14 million today) to support the museum. It specifically stated that the art collection should be exhibited "for the education and enjoyment of the public forever." She went on to say that if her wishes were not honored, the property and collection should be sold and the profits donated to Harvard University ("Isabella Stewart Gardner Museum," *Wikipedia*).

The Hefty Heist

In the early hours of March 18, 1980, the two thieves disguised as Boston police officers were patiently sitting in their hatchback, which was parked near the Gardner Museum. A small group of late-night partygoers who happened to be nearby noticed the two uniformed officers in their vehicle—so they decided to drive off. Shortly before 1:00 a.m.,

Richard Abath, who was one of the security guards, had just completed his tour inside the museum.

It is shortly after 1:00 a.m. when the two disguised cops leave their hatchback and walk briskly and directly to the side entrance of the museum. After one of them presses the buzzer, Abath responds through an intercom. One of the men answers, "Police. Let us in. We heard about a disturbance in the courtyard."

Abath, who is sitting at the control desk, looks at the video screens and notices that the two men are in uniform. Since two false alarms went off earlier that night at the museum, Abath and his partner guard, Randy Hestand, were a little on edge. While they had orders not to admit anyone into the museum, Abath seemed convinced that the police are responding to a legitimate call and decides to buzz the men through two sets of locked doors—it is 1:24 a.m.

Once inside, one of the thieves asks Abath if anyone else is on guard duty. When Abath tells him about his partner who is making his rounds, he is ordered to call Hestand on his walkie-talkie to come to the front desk. Meanwhile, one of the intruders tricks Abath to move away from the control station by asking him for his identification since they have a warrant for his arrest. In doing so, Abath leaves his desk, which had the only alarm button in the museum designed to immediately alert the police.

When Hestand shows up, one of the men quickly begins to handcuff him; at the same time, the other thief is handcuffing Abath. The intruders made sure that both guards were away from the control desk before they secured their hands. "This is a robbery," one of them said, "Don't give us any problems and you won't get hurt." After each guard is hastily wrapped around the head with duct tape—making sure his mouth and eyes are covered—they lead them down to the basement, where both are secured to pipe fixtures.

The thieves now have the museum all to themselves and are ready to go to work—it is 1:48 a.m. They head upstairs and quickly go to the Dutch Room, intending to take the large Rembrandt paintings first. As they approach the artworks, an alarm goes off which startles them—but they do not panic. They realize that the motion detector went off, which is what happens when visitors approach too close to the paintings, so they quickly destroy the apparatus.

And now they begin their thievery. They quickly cut Rembrandt's *The Storm on the Sea of Galilee* (64 × 51 inches) and *A Lady and Gentleman in Black* (52 × 43 inches) from their frames. Then they take Vermeer's *The Concert* (29 × 26 inches); some art dealers say it could bring as much as $300 million. Next they steal Govaert Flinck's *Landscape with an Obelisk* (22 × 28 inches). The thieves now grab a very small self-portrait of Rembrandt along with a bronze Chinese beaker or Ku (twelve inches tall) that dates back to the Shang Dynasty (1120–1100 BCE). It is somewhat of a mystery why they chose to take the Ku as the last piece.

At around 1:51 a.m., they swiftly move to another area and take five Degas illustrations from their frames; the smallest was 6 × 8 inches and the largest was 12 × 9.5 inches. Then something catches the eye of one of the men, and for some odd reason (considering all the valuable art work available to them), he tries to take a Napoleonic banner above the entry to the Tapestry Room. After spending some time removing a number of small screws that held the banner to the frame, he becomes impatient and pulls off the ten-inch gilded eagle finial from the top of the flagpole and settles for that. The Manet's *Chez Tortoni* (10 × 13 inches), which was in the Blue Room, was the last portrait stolen.

Before leaving, the thieves visit the two guards in the basement to make sure they would stay secured all night. Meanwhile, Abath optimistically hums Bob Dylan's forlorn ballad "I Shall Be Released" to calm himself down. The guards are relieved when the thieves simply check them out and leave.

The intruders return to the main floor and destroy the video recorders that filmed them as they entered the museum. They also proceed to remove the data printouts, which recorded them as they carried out their thievery. At 2:41 a.m., the two men carry part of their loot to their vehicle; it took them two trips to haul everything out. It was 2:45 a.m. when they closed the door to the museum: the big heist was completed in a relatively short period of time. The authorities do not know for certain whether the thieves had one or two vehicles available to haul away the stolen art.

About four hours later, two security guards arrived to relieve Abath and Hestand, but they are unable to enter the building. One of the guards then called his supervisor who had a master key; when he shows up, all three enter the museum only to find that a robbery has taken place. The supervisor called Lyle Grindle, who was the security chief of the museum: Lyle told him to immediately call the police and also notify Anne Hawley, the director of the museum, of the theft (Kurkjian 2016).

The Investigation

Dan Falzon headed up a team of almost thirty FBI agents to investigate the case. In reviewing the crime scene, it was obvious that the thieves did not seem to be respectful of the precious art they stole: they hacked two Rembrandts. In short, their conduct did not suggest that they were professional art thieves.

But why did they not steal other valuable drawings like Titian's *Rape of Europa*, arguably the most valuable painting in Boston, or Michelangelo's prized *Piea* that were there for the taking? And why spend the time it took to rip off the finial shaped like an eagle? Was it taken as a souvenir from the biggest art heist in history? Furthermore, the thieves simply passed by a Botticelli and two Raphael paintings. Did they have a "prepared hit list," which was handed to them by someone?

The intruders were cunning and fearless and knew that they did not have to hurry. They seemed confident and had knowledge of the museum's security system. The two men wore gloves and were careful not to leave any physical evidence behind. They did, however, not seem to mind that the guards had a good look at them.

When questioned about their appearance, the guards told the police that one of the men was in his late thirties and about five feet nine inches tall. They said he had a slim build and wore gold wire glasses; his moustache, however, appeared to be fake. The second thief seemed to be in his early thirties. He had a stocky build with heavy cheeks, and he also had a moustache.

The Two Art Thieves

In the beginning, there was suspicion that the two guards might have been involved in the robbery. Abath, who dropped out of Berklee College of Music, took the job to earn a little money, since the midnight shift didn't require any physical work. He would often perform with a local band at night and get to the museum shortly before midnight. It was a boring job, and most of the time Abath would read and do various mundane things to pass the time—always waiting for the dawn and the end of a long, tiresome night.

He admitted to the authorities that on other occasions some drinking had gone on in the museum while he was on duty. He also said that in the past he had smoked marijuana before going to work, which was more of an issue twenty-five years ago. The guards were also given polygraphs. While Hestand passed the examination, Abath's results were inconclusive; however, they were both eventually cleared of any involvement in the heist.

The FBI team spent considerable time interviewing present and past employees. They talked to many suspects and others who may have had some connection to the intruders—but they found nothing. Agents also traveled to a number of foreign countries following up leads that came in; but there were no solid clues that led anywhere.

In the beginning, the investigators thought that the thieves had several accomplices to assist them. The thirteen pieces of stolen artwork, which were mostly in canvas form, however, were not too difficult to carry out to their vehicle in two trips.

It appears most likely that the two men posing as police officers the partygoers saw in their hatchback were the only ones involved in the heist.

There were thousands of tips and leads that poured in since a $5 million reward was announced for information leading to the recovery of the art in good condition; however, those calls mostly ended up in frustration. Then at one point, investigators discovered that the postage-stamp-size etching of Rembrandt that the robbers took had been stolen from the museum twenty years earlier in 1970 but was then recovered from an art dealer who said he got it from a syndicate character. It happened when a visitor at the museum created a disturbance in the Dutch Room, and during the confusion he pocketed the etching.

In 2005, when a reporter at the Boston Globe interviewed Abath—under the protection of anonymity—he disclosed that he took alcohol and marijuana prior to his work duties. Furthermore, in a more recent interview, Abath admitted to also taking LSD and cocaine.

In March 2005, Anne Hawley released a statement regarding the theft for the first time: part of that statement addressed one promising lead.

On the occasion of the 15th anniversary of the theft, I call out to an important person to us. Years ago, I received a lead from a sincere individual giving me information that was comforting and genuine. The person clearly was concerned about the stolen art and knew its condition. We acted in good faith and complied with the first request. I'm very much hoping that this person will contact me again by writing or calling, or through our Security Director. Contact information is available on our website gardnermuseum.org/information/theft.asp. I assure complete confidentially.

Hawley's statement also pointed out that the stolen items should be stored at seventy degrees Fahrenheit and 50 percent humidity to protect the integrity of the art. A reward of $5 million is still offered for information leading to the return of the stolen art in good condition. (Kurkjian 2005).

Please contact the director of security of the museum at 617-278-5114 or the FBI at 617-742-5533. Images of the art are available at gardnermuseum.org/information/theft.asp

Two Art Detectives

In Ulrich Boser's well-researched book *The Gardner Heist*, he paid tribute to Harold Smith, who was a well-known investigator and detective who represented Lloyds of London and numerous other insurance companies for over a half century, pursuing fine art and jewelry theft. Smith had a shrewd mind when it came to recovering stolen art, and throughout his career he solved his share of important art heists.

Smith was obsessed by the master theft of the thirteen artworks from the Gardner Museum and devoted many years to the case. In his 2009 book, Boser presents an in-depth account of the numerous leads that Smith traced down in his vain quest to recover the paintings. Smith died in 2005, with the case still unsolved.

In that same year, journalist Boser took up the gauntlet: he began his own search for the Gardner stolen art:

> I went back to my case files. I had been working the caper for more than three years and added hundreds of pages of documents, search warrants, informant reports, trial transcripts and witness statements. I had uncovered snapshots of more than two-dozen suspects.

All told, Boser conducted two hundred interviews and visited twelve different states and four countries in his search for the Gardner art. In his book he described in detail his years of fruitless searching and cutting deals with master art thieves, drug dealers, and gangsters trying to get information; there were, however, no fruitful leads.

Boser is, however, to be commended for his diligence and resource-fulness in attempting to track down the Gardner stolen art—even though it is still out there somewhere. He said, "My dream, though, was not to understand the theft—it was to return the lost art. But that too seemed a mystery" (Boser 2009).

Out There Somewhere

In some cases, masterworks that have been stolen from other museums have been recovered even after many years. Investigators and directors of museums, however, have been disappointed and baffled that the Gardner art has not been recovered. The museum continues to hang several of the empty frames to remind visitors of their stolen masterpieces.

Empty Frames Still Hang in the Gardner Museum

The 1994 Crime Act extended the five-year statute of limitations on interstate transportation of stolen property and receiving stolen goods across state lines to twenty years. According to Boser:

The law also made it a federal crime to steal, receive or dispose of any cultural object worth more than $100,000, and while

Congress passed the law after the heist, it could be used to convict someone who handles the masterpieces today. "The crime
is handling the stolen works or concealing them and that can
happen at any time," art theft lawyer Bob Goldman told me.
"If someone buys the Gardner Rembrandt fifty years down the
road, they can still be prosecuted under this law."

Since the statute of limitations has run out for prosecuting the thieves,
it could increase the chances of the artwork being recovered. The US attorney in Boston stated that he would not prosecute anyone who offers
to return the paintings. Unless the heist involved organized crime, the
actual thieves might someday find that their desire to boast outweighs
their fear of retaliation from those who commissioned the theft. Or, we
can so hope, anyway.

FBI Update

In 2014, FBI special agent Geoff Kelly, the lead investigator in the
Gardner heist, told WFXT-TV that he has identified three persons of
interest in the robbery: Carmello Merlino, Robert Guarente, and Robert
Gentile—all with connections to organized crime. He also stated that
reliable sources have informed them of confirmed sightings of the stolen Gardner art years after the heist.

Kelly said that in the 1990s, several FBI informants told the bureau
that Merlino had intentions of returning Rembrandt's *Storm on the Sea of
Galilee* to collect the reward. But then, Merlino and his associates were
arrested on another charge, and the painting was never recovered.

Kelly thinks that Guarente at some point handed over the Gardner
art to Gentile, who had connections to the mob in Philadelphia. Gentile,
in turn, was instrumental in transporting all or a portion of the art to
Philadelphia, where it was seen and put up for sale in 2000.

Merlino and Guarente have since died, and Gentile has denied knowing anything about the missing paintings. If this is right, there seems to
be little hope of Gentile talking unless he's about to be convicted of

some other serious offence and decides to take the risk of turning informant (Ward 2014).

According to Anthony Amore, security head and chief investigator at the Gardner Museum, the latest development in the long investigation resulted from a tip a caller made to the authorities in 2010. And in 2013, he pointed out that the tip was so helpful it led to the identities of the three men of interest mentioned by Kelly and allowed the tracing of the art from Boston to Connecticut and Philadelphia. Armore said, "I do believe there are people out there who can give us information that will get us to the paintings" (FBI Has Confirmed Sightings of the Gardner Artwork 2014).

A Journalist Detective

Stephen Kurkijan, a superb journalist, has won three Pulitzer Prizes as a *Boston Globe* investigative reporter. His revelatory book *Master Thieves*, which was published in 2015, is a gripping account of researching the Gardner art theft for almost twenty years. His book is an intensive attempt to crack the case by reconsidering the evidence. He pointed out that the Gardner case "was beset by carelessly blown leads and missed opportunities, raising the question of whether it was most effective for the FBI to be solely responsible for leading it." While his investigations took him deep into the gangster world in an attempt to recover the stolen art, the FBI agents who worked painstaking on the case did not penetrate the underworld in their attempt to recover the artwork.

Kurkijan wrote, "Just like the Boston police, and many others who'd tried to help over the years, ultimately I had to cede jurisdiction to the FBI. Thus far, they had been unwilling to act on my information. I had to stop there."

Another FBI Update

In March 2015, the FBI finally identified the two thieves who committed the art heist. The two criminals were identified as George Reissfelder and Lenny DiMuzio. It is of interest to note that Secretary of State John Kerry was successful in getting Reissfelder's first-degree murder conviction overturned in 1982. "We got justice," Kerry told a reporter in 2009 of his work for the notorious hoodlum, "and I'll go to my grave proud that we did."

Only one year after the record robbery, both thieves were dead. Reissfelder died from an overdose of drugs, but the authorities were skeptical about the cause of his death, while DiMuzio was murdered in the world of organized crime.

The FBI decided to confirm the identities of the two thieves on the twenty-fifth anniversary of the crime. The authorities believe that Merlino arranged the audacious heist for Reissfelder and DiMuzio. It is not clear, however, if Merlino was operating on his own or was working for someone else.

Journalist Howie Carr wrote that Kerry seemed nonchalant when speaking to US News in 2009 with possible loss of the invaluable art. "I don't know if those paintings ended up on eBay," he quipped, "but they're not on my wall" (Carr 2015).

In August 2015, the authorities released a fuzzy surveillance video from the eve of the 1990 Boston art heist in an appeal to the public to help them recover the valuable artworks: it is the first time the video has been released. The vehicle in the video was similar to the one reportedly seen parked outside the museum on the night of the theft. In the video, a man exited the car and proceeded to the side door and pressed the buzzer.

The tape shows Abath doing a rather strange thing: he opened the side door of the museum and then allowed a man to enter. The shadowy figure in the video that entered the museum spent several minutes in the reception area, where he handed Abath a document of some sort before leaving. Was the mystery man not only checking out the museum but also involved in setting up the heist? (Mashberg 2015).

Boston attorney George Burke said that he received a call from a former client who stated that he recognized the dark figure in the short grainy video. Burke reported that he contacted the US attorney's office, telling them that his client was agreeable to cooperate with the authorities provided that he would remain anonymous.

The authorities said that the mystery man who entered the museum was not one of the two suspects who carried out the heist—they are both now deceased. By releasing the video, they are reaching out to the public for their help in recovering the stolen artwork.

When US attorney Carmen M. Ortiz, who took over the case several years ago, was asked if the tape had been reviewed twenty-five years ago, she said, "I can't answer that" and asked to check with the FBI. Peter Kowenhoven, the FBI's assistant special agent in charge in Boston, said, "It may have been reviewed back then, I'm not sure of the answer to that question." He then went on to say the he was now concentrating on whether the video would pick up any new clues.

JonPaul Kroger, who trained Abath for the security guard position, pointed out that Abath was not reliable: he was often late for work; other times he would phone and say that he was ill or had too much to drink. Kroger also maintained that Abath was told to take the names and badge numbers of any police officers if they requested permission to enter and then contact the Boston police headquarters to confirm that they had been sent to the museum.

Abath said that the thieves didn't need any help from him since they knew very well what they were doing. And in 2013, he told the Boston Globe that FBI agents had grilled him about the robbery the previous year since he had been suspected of being involved in the heist for a long time.

Abath was at a loss to explain how the motion detectors only recorded his footsteps in the Blue Room the night of the theft where the Manet was stolen. The detectors, however, recorded all the footsteps of the two thieves that night inside the museum, but there was no evidence that the thieves had entered the Blue Room.

In his detailed book, Kurkijan wrote:

In 2010 Abath was called before a grand jury, where he admitted to investigators that he prided himself on being able to avoid having his footsteps picked up on the motion detector equipment by "duck walking" through a gallery like rocker Chuck Berry. But he insisted he had had nothing to do with the thieves or the theft itself, and reminded the grand jurors that he had remained duct-taped and handcuffed in the basement the entire night.

Abath, who is now in his fifties, is living in Vermont, where he is employed as a teacher's aide. He has repeatedly denied that he was involved in the robbery. In all the interviews he had with the FBI, he never mentioned admitting the mystery man to the museum the previous night of the heist. He did, however, say that on his last day of work at the museum he handed in his two-week notice that he was quitting his job as security guard.

In 2016, the FBI searched Robert Gentile's home for the third time while Gentile was in jail awaiting trial for firearms offenses. Four years earlier, when the authorities searched his home they found a handwritten list of the art that was stolen in the Gardner Museum heist, a note estimating the value of the art, and some police uniforms.

The authorities also the revealed that in 2015 they recorded Gentile speaking to an undercover FBI agent, telling him that he was able to arrange a deal to sell two of the stolen art pieces for $500,000 each.

Gentile's lawyer, Ryan McGuigan, stated that Gentile "has denied any involvement for the past four years with the theft. He has also denied possessing or ever having possessed any of the paintings" (Thomson 2016).

While FBI agents thoroughly went through Gentile's home with search dogs and also dug up the ground around his home, they apparently came up with nothing. Even some leads from other mobsters did not provide any significant information. The empty frames still hang in the Gardner Museum.

Conclusion

The two fake cops—Reissfelder and DiMuzio—did little to gain entrance to the museum, but on the other hand, they got away with much.

They had enough time to make off with a $1 billion worth of art treasures. They seemed to know, however, what paintings they were after. While they took some masterpieces, they ignored other valuable paintings that were there for the taking. It suggests that the intruders had a shopping list that someone prepared for them.

The two thieves posing as police officers in their vehicle were the only ones seen by witnesses very early that morning near the Gardner Museum. The two men had a plan: get in, take what they were looking for, and get out. They were bold and efficient—they carried out the largest heist ever, and they did it all by themselves.

Once they had their booty, the thieves most likely drove to a prearranged designation outside the city. They handed over the stolen artwork to someone (call him person S); the two men departed swiftly and had nothing more to do with handling the stolen art.

Person S did not have a way to immediately dispose of the art. He did not want to work a deal with the museum for the reward because he wanted to keep his identity unknown, and furthermore he didn't trust the FBI. He did, however, have connections with the syndicate. It's most likely he transferred the art to organized crime members Carmello Merlino, Robert Guarente, and Robert Gentile, whom FBI agent Kelly identified as persons of interest in the Gardner case.

There were no money transactions as the art was passed through various hands until contact was made with a buyer. The entire loot taken from the Gardner heist, however, was too large to dispose of in a one transaction, so the thirteen stolen artworks were divided up among various parties. Nevertheless, it was still difficult to find buyers, since they would probably only offer pennies on the dollar for the stolen art.

According to agent Kelly, some art was taken to Philadelphia, where it was up for sale in 2000. Since credible sightings of the art have been confirmed, we think that there is very little chance that any of the paintings might have been transported to a foreign country. The paintings, while damaged during the robbery, have probably deteriorated to some extent due to poor handling and storage.

It is baffling that the paintings have not shown up during all these twenty-six years. Some vicious, greedy, and cruel people out there who have purchased most of the stolen art are holding on to them—and mocking the art world.

We hope, however, that someday some of the paintings will finally be returned and displayed in the Gardner Museum for millions to see and admire—but for now, it remains the greatest art heist mystery of all time.

The Caper and Collusion in the Castle

It is 1907 and Oklahoma just becomes the forty-sixth state admitted to the Union. The RMS *Lusitania* arrives in New York City after a five-day record crossing of the Atlantic. Finland is the first European country to give women the right to vote. The first cabs with taximeters begin operating in London, and England's King Edward VII and Queen Alexandra are on their way to visit Ireland.

But, then, just four days before the king's official visit, the Irish Crown Jewels mysteriously disappear from within the Dublin Castle's granite walls.

The authorities, led by Scotland Yard, expose a complex web of collusion, secrecy, and scandal. Sir Arthur Vicars, the overseer and protector of the jewels, and his staff, including his live-in partner, the charismatic Frank Shackleton (brother of the famous Antarctica explorer), are thoroughly scrutinized.

The investigation uncovers a circle of deeply closeted gay men within the Dublin Castle itself. The cabal includes Vicars, Shackleton, Lord Haddo, son of the viceroy Lord Aberdeen, and the duke of Argyll, the king's brother-in-law. Their highly scandalous behavior (for the times) quickly reaches the newspapers and threatens to become a major international incident.

More than a century has passed: the theft has never been solved and the Irish Crown Jewels were never recovered. It remains one of the most bizarre and puzzling mysteries in Irish criminal history.

Background

The Irish Crown Jewels were presented to the Order of St. Patrick in Ireland by England's King William IV in 1830 and were to be worn by the lord lieutenant of Ireland on ceremonial occasions.

The ornate jewels consisted of a Star and a Badge along with collars of five Knights of Order. The large eight-pointed star was made of Brazilian diamonds with eight star-points and a center shamrock consisting of emeralds and a cross of rubies in the center with a blue enamel background. The badge also had emerald shamrocks and a ruby red cross, which was surrounded by blue enamel with rose and more Brazilian diamonds. While the Irish Crown Jewels were not the equivalent in value of the English Crown Jewels (probably worth several billion dollars), they were valued to be worth at least several million dollars today.

On May 4, 1907, the Irish International Exhibition (Ireland's World Fair) opened in Herbert Park, Dublin. Later in the summer on July 10, members of the Royal Family, King Edward VII and Queen Alexandra and Princess Victoria, visited the exhibition.

In the intervening two months, the Irish Crown Jewels disappeared. The king was "not amused" by the news; after all, the jewels were a gift from King William almost four decades ago: Queen Victoria and Edward VII, however, were the only two monarchs to avail themselves of the jewels during their visit to Ireland.

The Audacious Theft

In 1903, the Irish Crown Jewels were transferred to a safe, which was then to be placed in the strong room in the Office of Arms in Dublin Castle. The three-foot-wide safe, however, was too large to be moved through the narrow door of the strong room. Sir Arthur Vicars, who was the custodian of the jewels, decided to place the safe in the office library. Vicars, who was fond of showing the Crown Jewels to visitors,

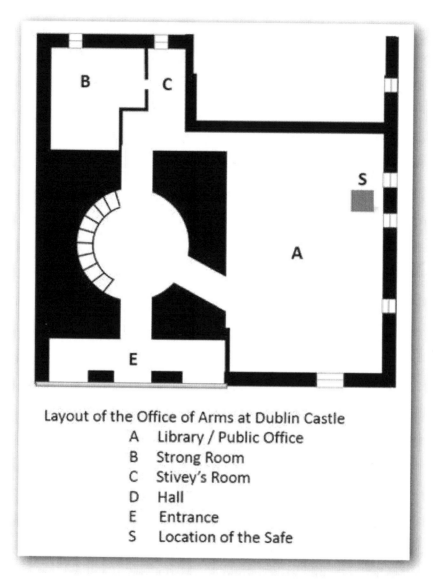

Layout of the Office of Arms at Dublin Castle

A   Library / Public Office
B   Strong Room
C   Stivey's Room
D   Hall
E   Entrance
S   Location of the Safe

especially enjoyed displaying them to women. But then, women seem to appreciate valuable jewelry much more than men (though in more recent times, things are a-changing). On June 11, 1907, Vicars showed the jewels to his friend John Crawford Hodgson, librarian to the Duke of Northumberland, who was visiting Ireland. It was the last time they were displayed in public.

6 July 1907,
Ireland Calling
Irish Crown Jewels stolen

Ireland Calling

This image was published by the RIC and the Dublin Metropolitan Police twice a week after the theft of the jewels was discovered.

ireland-calling.com

Early Wednesday morning on July 3, Mrs. Mary Farrell, who cleaned the Office at Arms, found the front-door entrance unlocked. She reported the incident to William Stivey, the messenger in the Office of Arms, who arrived at around 10:00 a.m. When Vicars arrived somewhat later that morning, Stivey informed him of what Mrs. Farrell told him about the front door being unlocked. Surprisingly, Vicars dismissed Stivey's comments about what Mrs. Farrell had told him and showed little interest in the matter.

When Mrs. Farrell arrived for work on Saturday morning July 6, she was surprised that the door of the strong room was now ajar, since it should have been locked. She then took note of the two keys in the lock on the inside grille: she took the two grille keys, locked the strong room, and left a note for Stivey. When Stivey arrived later and read Mrs. Farrell's note, he became quite concerned and anxiously waited for Vicars to show up. When Stivey reported the matter to Vicars, he was astonished that Vicars again seemed unconcerned.

Around 2:30 that Saturday afternoon, Vicars handed Stivey a piece of jewelry along with the key and asked him to deposit the item in the safe. As Stivey approached the safe, he was surprised to see that it was unlocked. When he realized the safe was empty, he was stunned and immediately called out to Vicars. When Vicars examined the safe, he, too, was astonished to discover that the Crown Jewels had been stolen. He quickly turned toward Stivey and told him to notify the authorities (Dungan 2003).

Sir Arthur Vicars

The Investigation

Superintendent John Lowe, of the Metropolitan Police, along with his assistant commissioner William Harrel and detective Owen Kerr, arrived at the scene and began the initial investigation.

They learned that seven people had keys to the front-door entrance to the Office of Arms: Arthur Vicars; William Stivey; Mr. Burtchaell, secretary; Mr. P. G. Mahony (Vicars's nephew), Cork Herald; Detective Kerr, the night inspector; Mrs. Farrell; and John O'Keeffe, whose job during the Dublin Season was to climb each night to light the lantern above the Bedford Tower. Since the Dublin Season ended late in March, O'Keeffe convinced the police that he had not entered the Office of Arms.

There were four keys to the outer door of the strong room: while three of them were with Vicars, Stivey, and Mahony, the fourth, previously owned by Burtchaell, was now kept in an unlocked drawer in the strong room. In addition, there were also two keys to the inside grille.

Vicars, on the other hand, held the only two keys to the safe; he carried one on his person and kept the other in his bedroom at his home. The lock experts who were called in stated that the safe lock has not been tampered with and was opened with its own key or possibly a copy of the original, but not by one made from a wax impression.

Mrs. Farrell told detective Owen about the entrance door having been left open Wednesday morning, and she revealed that on Saturday also she found the strong room door slightly open. Mrs. Farrell also mentioned that several months prior to the robbery, she saw an intruder in the library office. She identified the person as Lord Haddo, the son of Lord Aberdeen. Lord Haddo, however, was not entitled to have access to the Office of Arms.

The police were wondering why Vicars and his staff had not mentioned anything about the two occasions that Mrs. Farrell found the two doors unlocked. They concluded that if Vicars had locked the safe as he said he had, it then appeared that someone has access to his keys or, perhaps, Vicars had left the safe unlocked. The authorities, however, drew a blank when they checked with locksmiths to see if anyone had a key made that would fit the safe or strong room.

A small piece of ribbon was neatly and carefully left behind in a red morocco case, which held the jewels. The ribbon had been attached to the badge with a clasp and fastened with very small screws: it would have taken about ten minutes to remove the ribbon without damaging it. Since the thief left the remaining material in the safe in neat order, it appeared that a person familiar with the layout of the Dublin Castle had committed the crime, rather than a thief who only wanted to secure his booty and get away fast.

Early on, the police cleared Mrs. Farrell, Stivey, and the office secretary Miss Gibbon as possible suspects. Vicars's two assistants George Burtehaell and Mr. Horlock were also ruled out since they had legitimate alibis.

By July 10, an irate King Edward VII had arrived in Dublin, but the ceremonial investiture plans were hastily postponed. Two days later, Inspector John Kane of Scotland Yard was brought in to assist in the investigation. Kane's report was not made public, but authors John Cafferky and Kevin Hannafin in *Scandal & Betrayal* wrote: "Kane exposed Sir Arthur's homosexual court and its ties to Lord Gower's circle in London. [The] report mentioned that Vicars associated closely with Lord Gower and his coterie of London gentlemen." That is, there was a homosexual circle within the castle itself.

> There is strong circumstantial evidence to link the four heralds to scandalous parties, which was said to have taken place at Dublin Castle. [Much later], *the Irish Times* printed an article alleging that Lord Haddo, son of the viceroy, Lord Aberdeen, made many visits to the Castle, and may well have participated in the heralds' "orgies." (O'Riordan 2001)

The four heralds were: Francis Bennett Goldney, mayor of Canterbury; Pierce O'Mahony, half-brother of Vicars; Francis Shackleton, Vicars's co-tenant; and Richard Gorges, a rogue and intimate friend of Shackleton. In *The Stealing of the Irish Crown Jewels: An Unsolved Crime*, author Myles Dungan wrote: "[Francis] Shackleton was a known homosexual and that he was probably sleeping with the king's brother-in-law, the Duke of Argyll."

Vicars was headstrong and determined to hold his ground and decided not to cooperate with the authorities from the very beginning. While there were whispers and rumors about his homosexual friends and possibly his own homosexuality, he refused to resign as Ulster King of Arms. (At the beginning of the twentieth century, homosexuality was considered to be a perversion and not an inclination or orientation.)

Meanwhile, King Edward VII was becoming more annoyed that the jewels had not been recovered and also that a potential scandal was brewing. The king wanted Vicars dismissed, so on October 23, Vicars was informed that his services as Ulster King of Arms were no longer required. Vicars was adamant and refused to resign his position; he was even offered a pension to resign, but he turned down the offer.

Since the authorities did not assign a lead investigator to the case, the "thorough" investigation promised by the Dublin police did not materialize. Haphazard questioning by different officers led to a lack of focus, and very little was accomplished (Dungan 2003).

The Puny Inquiry

On January 6, 1908, the king advised Lord Aberdeen to appoint a commission to investigate the theft and also to determine Vicars's role since he was the custodian of the jewels. The commission held its first meeting on January 10.

Vicars and his supporters objected to the private nature of the investigation. They maintained that the inquiry should be public and also be authorized to require witnesses to be under oath. Since the commissioners held that the inquiry would be private, Vicars, ever steadfast, chose not to cooperate and did not show up since he felt that he would not have the opportunity to vindicate himself. The press sided with Vicars and criticized the administration for conducting a secret inquiry. The commission, however, held firm and proceeded to carry out their investigation.

Here are some comments from individuals that the commission interviewed:

Goldney stated that Vicars requested a sum of money from him to cover a financial commitment he was unable to pay. Vicars explained that the money was for Shackleton, who was seriously in debt.

Chief Inspector Kane then reviewed the tidy manner and the time it took for the thief to remove the ribbon and tiny screws from the jewelry. He concluded that it appeared to be an "inside" job. Kane was not asked; nor did he volunteer whom he named as the thief in his report; it was a typical example of how the commission conducted the inquiry.

Shackleton confirmed his living arrangements with Vicars: they were cotenants. When the commissioners questioned Shackleton about his financial difficulties, he stated that his money problems had no bearing in the inquiry; furthermore, he did not wish the matter to be leaked to the press.

When Shackleton was asked if he had access at any time to the keys in Vicars's home, he calmly replied that he had many opportunities to take the keys but he denied stealing them or that he knew anything about the missing jewels. He denied everything.

Shackleton was known to be friends with Captain Richard Gorges, who served in the army during the Boer War. Gorges was a rogue who lived hard and drank heavily: he was in debt and also had a checkered background.

The commission completed their investigation in six days and interviewed twenty-two people. All were cleared, but Goldney and Shackleton; however, both of them were out of the country in late June and early July but were due in Dublin for King Edward's visit.

Although Vicars was cleared, a central passage in the commission's report seems to us to be more of a "slap on the wrist" rather than a condemnation.

> Having fully investigated all the circumstances connected with the loss of the Regalia of the Order of St. Patrick, and having examined and considered carefully the arrangements of the Office of Arms in which the Regalia were deposited, and the provisions made by Sir Arthur Vicars, or under his direction for their safe keeping, and having regard especially to the inactivity of Sir Arthur Vicars on the occasion immediately preceding the disappearance of the jewels, when he knew that the Office and the Strong Room had been opened at night by unauthorized persons, we feel bound to report to Your Excellency that, in our opinion, Sir Arthur Vicars did not exercise due vigilance or proper care as the custodian of the Regalia. (Cafferky and Hannafin 2002)

The commission listened to many inconsequential comments and did not focus on relevant issues and evidence. The commissioner's inquiry was a whitewash and did not investigate the theft, but it concentrated on whether Vicars had taken proper care of the jewels. Apparently King Edward managed to suppress a detailed inquiry into the scandalous behavior in the Castle.

Earlier, Pierce O'Mahony, half brother of Vicars, who campaigned for a public meeting to vindicate Vicars, suggested that Shackleton and an accomplice were responsible for the theft, even though Shackleton was in England at the time. The king, however, was not interested: the entire staff of the Chief's Herald was forced to resign, and Vicars was ousted from his office.

A Scenario for the Theft

Francis Shackleton first met Sir Arthur Vicars in 1897, when Vicars appointed Shackleton to the position assistant secretary in the Office of Arms. In 1900, Shackleton left to serve in the Boer War for the next several years. He was a high-spirited person who had a zest for life: he was always optimistic that his next fortune was just around the corner.

In 1905, Vicars appointed him Dublin Herald, and shortly afterward he and Vicars decided to live together. Shackleton's business ventures soon got him in debt, and he needed money: he had a motive, the opportunity, and he formulated a plan whereby he would get out of debt. Shackleton decided to steal the Irish Crown Jewels with the aid of an accomplice, Captain Richard Gorges, with whom he was most likely involved in a homosexual relationship. Shackleton, who admitted that he had access to Vicars's keys, took Vicars's safe key, which he kept at home, and made a duplicate copy. On the other hand, it was easier to get hold of the key to the front door and the strong room since various people held those keys.

On June 7, 1907, Shackleton left Dublin and went to England for one month. The plan was for Gorges to steal the Crown Jewels while Shackleton was out of the country. The last time the jewels were seen in public was on June 11, which is when the formal announcement was made that King Edward VII was going to visit Ireland.

One night prior to July 2, Gorges entered the Office of Arms. He used the duplicate safe key he got from Shackleton to open the safe. He knew he had time to neatly and carefully separate the ribbon and the small screws from the jewels, and he just walked off with the loot. He purposely left the front door open so that the theft would be discovered. Shackleton then planned to return to Dublin shortly before the king arrived on July 10 but definitely after the theft of the jewels had been announced.

Even though Vicars had been informed that Mrs. Farrell found the front door open on July 3, the crime had not been reported since Vicars was not aware that the Crown Jewels had been stolen. Shackleton now became anxious and quite concerned: if the theft was not discovered until the day the king arrived, he would not have an alibi since he would already be in Dublin.

Shackleton and Gorges decided to make it more obvious that someone had entered the Office of Arms without authority. Gorges returned and left the strong room door open, trying to force the discovery that a robbery had taken place so that Shackleton would have an alibi. What more could they do? On July 6, the missing jewels were finally discovered by accident when Vicars asked Stivey to place a piece of jewelry in the safe. Shackleton, then decided to return to Dublin on July 9, and the very next day King Edward began his official visit.

We think that the authorities did not have sufficient evidence to convict Shackleton and Gorges; but then, it's fair to ask if they did all they could to solve the crime? It is also likely that Shackleton and Gorges escaped conviction for their crime because of the threat of blackmail that might have involved the monarch of England. Even if Vicars was not involved in the actual theft, it is very hard to believe that he did not soon come to know the real truth.

While there have been theories, rumors, as well as hoaxes perpetrated over many years that the missing jewels have been found, nothing have ever surfaced on what happened to them. We think that the Crown Jewels have been dismantled and sold; but, then, someone may have them sequestered and are still intact, as they were the day they were stolen. And maybe that person (or, more likely, his descendant) removes the jewels from their secret hiding place and admires them, as others did so long ago. It's likely that we will never know the fate of the jewels.

Over a century has passed since the Irish Crown Jewels were stolen. The theft has never been solved and the Crown Jewels were never recovered. It is one of the great unsolved and baffling mysteries of Irish history. If, however, documents are discovered in the archives sometime in the future that identifies who took the missing jewels, we think it will turn out that we got it right.

Aftermath

As we shall see, quite a few of our main characters came to unhappy ends.

King Edward VII, who likely played a major role in the manner of how the inquiry was handled, died in 1910. Being conscious of the nature of prying historians, he ordered that his personal papers be burned in his will.

Chief Inspector John Kane retired from Scotland Yard in 1911 after thirty-seven years of service. He never disclosed in his report the name of the individual who he felt committed the crime.

Francis Bennett Goldney continued on as mayor of Canterbury until 1911. Then, in the general election he won a seat as an independent Unionist, which he held until his death in an automobile accident in France in 1918.

Lord Haddo, son of Lord Aberdeen, despite the many rumors about him, managed to escape the Crown Jewel scandal. In 1908, Augustine Birrell, chief secretary for Ireland, defended Lord Haddo in the House of Commons, stating that Lord Haddo lived in Scotland continuously from March through December 1907; but we believe Mrs. Farrell was correct when she told the police that she saw Haddo in the Office of Arms sometime in May 1907. He became an elder of the Church of Scotland and devoted his life to various local issues. He was married twice, outlived his two wives, and died in 1965.

Duke of Argyll, the king's brother-in-law, who had a dreadful reputation, also was not dishonored by the Crown Jewel fiasco. He died from pneumonia in 1914.

Pierce Mahony stayed on as Cork Herald, but then resigned in 1910; he was then called to the Bar in Dublin. In April 1914, he assisted Vicars with some legal matters. Several months later in July, he went out boating on a lake at his father's estate. When he did not return, a search party found his dead body partly submerged in the lake. He had been shot twice in chest with a shotgun. Oddly, his death was determined to be accidental. (Once might be an accident, but twice…) There were some, however, who thought that he might have found out who stole the Crown Jewels.

After King Edward VII died, Sir Arthur Vicars petitioned George V twice for a second inquiry, but cabinet members stymied his efforts. In 1913, however, he won a libel case against *London Mail*. Then in 1919, he married Gertrude Wright. In 1921, the Irish Republican Army (IRA) killed him during a raid on his house: they also burned down his residence. In his 1920 will, which was not fully made available to the public until 1976, he condemned the authorities and King Edward VII for shielding Shackleton, who was "the real culprit and thief."

Richard Gorges wandered off into the dark world of chronic alcoholism after the theft of the jewels. In 1914, he was commissioned a captain in the army but then discharged the following year. In July 1915, he killed detective Young and was sentenced to twelve years penal servitude for manslaughter. When he was released from prison, he was only able to survive with the support of his family until the 1950s, when life became so unbearable that he jumped in front of a train and ended his life.

Francis Shackleton's financial dealings ended in bankruptcy in August 1910; in 1912 he fled to Portuguese West Africa, where he was arrested. In 1913, he was sentenced to jail for fifteen months for fraud. After he was released from prison, he opened an antique shop. He died in St. Richard's Hospital in June 1944: he was sixty-four years old (Cafferky and Hannafin 2002).

Attorney for the Damned

On November 28, 1911, at around 9:00 a.m., the phone rings in the downtown Los Angeles office of one of America's most famous lawyers. The attorney who has agreed to defend the McNamara brothers who were arrested for the shocking bombing of the *Los Angeles Times* building quickly picks up the phone and has a brief conversation. He grabs his hat, leaves the building, and hastily proceeds south along Main Street.

Just two blocks away Bert Franklin, the defense team's chief investigator, has prearranged to meet with a juror at the corner of Third and Los Angeles Streets. His mission is to pay the juror $4,000 to vote not guilty in the bombing case.

Meanwhile, the district attorney's office has set up a sting operation since the juror reported the bribe to the police. But then, why is the prominent attorney so quick to hurry off in the direction where the illegal transaction is taking place? Was he tipped off, and is he now trying to attempt to stop the bribe?

After handing over the money to the juror, Franklin walked one block toward the attorney's office. Just as he is about to meet the attorney, who is waving his hat and striding toward him, the police step in and arrest Franklin.

Franklin pled guilty to the charge of bribing a juror; later, he testified that the defense attorney had knowledge of and also approved the bribery efforts.

The famous civil libertarian lawyer and champion of the downtrodden was none other than Clarence Darrow. He was arrested and charged with jury tampering. But, was Darrow innocent or guilty?

Background

Clarence Darrow was born in Kinsman, Ohio, on April 18, 1857. He grew up in an unconventional home. His father was an avid abolitionist, a fiery dissenter, and also an atheist. Darrow wrote: "The fact that my father was a heretic always put him on the defensive. We children thought it was only right and loyal that we should defend his cause." On the other hand, his mother was a staunch supporter of female suffrage and an advocate for women's rights. So it's not too surprising that Darrow continuously defended the downtrodden and vulnerable people in society.

Darrow enrolled at Allegheny College for a year and then attended the University of Michigan Law School; however, he did not graduate from either institution. While teaching at a district school for several years, he began to study law on his own. He then decided it would be more advantageous to get a job working in a law office. When he felt he was prepared, he took and passed the Ohio Bar examination and was admitted to the Ohio bar in 1878.

Clarence Darrow

Corporate Attorney to Labor Attorney

Darrow started working as a small-town lawyer and also became involved in politics. In 1880, he married Jessie Ohl, and then late in the 1880s, he moved to Chicago with his wife and son, Paul. In Chicago he often spoke openly on behalf of the Democratic Party and then ended up getting a position as an attorney for the city. After several years, he accepted a position as an attorney for the Chicago and North-Western Railway Company.

In 1894, he defended Eugene W. Debs, the head of the American Railway Union, who was prosecuted by the government for his leading role in the Pullman Strike. Even though Darrow took a financial hit, he broke with the railroad to represent Debs. While he successfully defended Debs in the first trial, Debs ended up in jail in the second trial.

In that same year he defended Patrick Eugene Prendergast, a newspaper distributor, who shot and killed Chicago mayor Carter H. Harrison. Sr. Prendergast then turned himself in to the police half an hour later. Darrow tried to show that his client was insane. It turned out to be the only murder-defense case of many throughout his entire career that Darrow lost, which ended in an execution.

In 1896, Darrow ran unsuccessfully for Congress as a Democrat. Meanwhile, his marriage was not going well and the following year he was divorced. In 1898, he joined the Anti-Imperialist League in opposing the US annexation of the Philippines. In that same year, he defended the woodworkers of Wisconsin in a well-known case: he also represented the United Mine workers in Pennsylvania in the huge anthracite coal strike in 1902. Two years later, Darrow married Ruby Hammerstrom, a young Chicago columnist.

From 1906 to 1907, Darrow defended three leaders of the Western Federation of Miners: William "Big Bill" Haywood (founder of the radical Industrial Workers of the World or "Wobblies") along with Charles Moyer and George Pettibone, who were arrested for murdering former Idaho governor Frank Steunenberg in 1905. After several trials, Haywood and Pettibone were acquitted and the charges against Moyer were dropped—but they may well have been guilty. J. Anthony Lukas's *Big Trouble: A Murder in a Small Western Town Sets Off a Struggle for the Soul of America* is a wonderful book on this astonishing case, which eventually engaged President Theodore Roosevelt and Supreme Court justice Oliver Wendell Holmes. It was clear: Darrow, the young defender, was on his way to becoming a great labor attorney.

In 1911, however, disaster struck and Darrow became involved in a major legal crisis, which we will discuss later. But first, we would like to tell you more about Darrow.

Some Famous Darrow Cases
Leopold and Loeb

In the summer of 1924, "little Bobby Franks," age fourteen, was looking forward to a nice dinner as he was walking home from school in the south side of Chicago. Not too far from his residence, which was in a wealthy neighborhood of the city, a car pulled up alongside of him and stopped. For some unknown reason, Bobby enters the car, but then, he never makes it home.

The very next day, a passing worker noticed Bobby's dead body lying in a culvert near the Indiana border. A pair of unusual horn-rimmed glasses that were found near the body linked the crime to Nathan Leopold; also, a ransom note, which had been typed on Leopold's typewriter, further confirmed his guilt. When Leopold, nineteen, and his friend Richard Loeb, eighteen, were confronted with the evidence, they confessed to the murder. Their wealthy parents immediately sought out Clarence Darrow to defend them.

Leopold, who was a brilliant law student at the University of Chicago, was planning to transfer to Harvard Law School. Loeb had already graduated from the University of Michigan and was also planning on attending law school. They both believed in Nietzsche's concept of the "superman." Inspired by a sense of nihilistic philosophy, they set out to commit what they felt was the perfect crime for the sheer excitement of getting away with it.

The newspapers in Chicago called the case "The Trial of the Century." The murder trial shocked the nation and is notable for the twelve-hour-long plea by Darrow to save his clients from the death penalty.

Several selections from Darrow's summation illustrate his rhetorical style:

> The tales of death were in their homes, their playgrounds, their schools; they were in the newspapers that they read; it was part of the common frenzy—what was life? It was nothing. It was the least sacred thing in existence and those boys were trained to this cruelty.
>
> You may hang these boys; you may hang them by the neck until they are dead. But in doing it will turn your face to the past. In doing it you are making it harder for every other boy who in ignorance and darkness must grope his way through the mazes which only childhood knows. (Darrow n.d.)

Darrow successfully persuaded Judge John Caverly to spare the lives of the two youthful killers; however, they both received life sentences in prison. Loeb was eventually murdered in prison in 1936. Leopold was finally released on parole in 1958: he died in Puerto Rico in 1971 at age sixty-six.

The Scopes Trial

In 1925, John T. Scopes, a high school teacher, was accused of violating Tennessee's Butler Act, which made it unlawful to teach evolution. The case often referred to as "The Monkey Trial" pitted Darrow, who was an avowed agnostic in religious matters, against William Jennings Bryan, who led the march to exclude Darwin's theory of evolution from classrooms in the United States. Broadly, the case reflected a clash of traditional beliefs and values with more contemporary ones.

Darrow and Bryan were fascinating men and drew significant attention to the case. The trial attracted hundreds of reporters from all over the nation and was the first trial to be broadcast on radio.

In the courtroom, Darrow faced an arduous fight. Judge John Raulston began every day with a prayer. He did not permit scientists to testify in favor of evolution, and furthermore, he refused to overrule the antievolution law.

The defense team was more concerned about defeating the Butler Act than just simply defending Scopes. Darrow became frustrated after debating Bryan for a week. He did, however, come up with an unusual plan: he called Bryan to the stand as an expert on the Bible. Since there were no summations in the trial, we have selected the following from the trial proceedings.

Darrow and Bryan

Comments and Quotations

Bryan criticizied the theory of evolution for teaching children that humans were but one of thirty-five thousand types of mammals and bemoaned the notion that human beings were descended "Not even from American monkeys, but from old world monkeys."

Bryan strongly stated that the purpose of Darwin's questioning was "to cast ridicule on everybody who believe in the Bible." Darrow replied, "We have the purpose of preventing bigots and ignoramuses from controlling the education in the United States."

Darrow used examples from the Book of Genesis to suggest that the stories of the Bible could not be scientific and should not be used in teaching science. He said, "You insult every man of science and learning in the world because he does not believe in your foolish religion" ("Scopes Trial," *Wikipedia*).

Darrow said, "Scopes isn't on trial; civilization is on trial." The prosecution, Darrow contended, was "opening the doors for a reign of bigotry equal to anything in the Middle Ages." He went on to say that the antievolution law made the Bible "the yardstick to measure every man's intellect, to measure every man's intelligence, to measure every man's learning" (Lindner n.d.).

Near the end of the trial, Darrow asked the jury to return a verdict of guilty, which meant that the case could then be appealed to the Tennessee Supreme Court. This procedural strategy by Darrow denied Bryan the opportunity for his long-prepared closing remarks, as well as his own final summation.

The jury deliberated for eight minutes and returned a verdict of guilty. On July 21, 1925, the judge ordered Scopes to pay a fine of one hundred dollars. One year later, the Tennessee Supreme Court overturned the verdict on a technicality. William Jennings Bryan died just one week after the trial.

The Tennessee law, however, would stand for forty-two more years; it wasn't until 1967 that the Butler Act was repealed.

Ossian Sweet

On September 8, 1925, Dr. Ossian Sweet, an African American doctor, moved his family into their new home in an all-white neighborhood in Detroit. That night, some 750 people assembled outside the Sweet home, outraged that a black family has moved into "their neighborhood."

The very next day an unruly white mob gathered about the Sweet home. In the confrontation that ensued that evening, one white man was killed from a shot that was fired from the upper floor in the Sweet residence.

Eleven blacks in the Sweet house were arrested and charged with murder. The NAACP contacted Darrow to represent Dr. Sweet and the other occupants in the upcoming trial. Darrow, however, was facing a twelve-man all-white jury.

First Trial: Darrow's Summation

If I thought any of you had any opinion about the guilt of my clients, I wouldn't worry, because that might be changed. What I'm worried about is prejudice. They are harder to change. They come with your mother's milk and stick like the color of the skin. I know that if these defendants had been a white group defending themselves from a colored mob, they never would have been arrested or tried. My clients are charged with murder, but they are really charged with being black.

The jury deliberated for forty-six hours, but they were unable to reach a verdict. Judge Frank Murphy declared a mistrial and dismissed the jury.

Second Trial: Darrow's Summation

How much do you know about prejudice? Race prejudice. Religious prejudice. These feelings that have divided men and caused them to do the most terrible things. Prejudices have burned men at the stake, broken them on the rack, torn every joint apart, destroyed people by the millions. Men have done this on account of some terrible prejudice, which even now is reaching out to undermine this republic of ours and to destroy the freedom that has been the most cherished part of our institutions. ("Darrow's Summations in the Sweet Trial" 1925–26)

The Verdict

After four hours, the jury returned a verdict of not guilty for Dr. Sweet's brother, Henry, who had fired the shot from the Sweet home. The prosecution then dismissed the charges against the ten other defendants. Darrow's summations are regarded as a landmark in the Civil Rights Movement. Dr. Ossian Sweet eventually committed suicide in 1960.

The Massie Trial

Thalia Massie, age twenty, told the police that it was shortly before 1:00 a.m. on September 13, 1931, when she had been abducted and raped by a group of young Hawaiian men. At the time, Thomas Massie, who was a lieutenant in the US Navy, and his wife, Thalia, were stationed at Pearl Harbor, Hawaii. The police quickly arrested and charged five Hawaiians with assaulting Thalia.

On December 6, the jury was unable to arrive at a verdict and the judge declared a mistrial. (Later, the charges against the five were dropped, and further investigation showed them to be innocent.)

Meanwhile, Thalia's mother, Grace Fortescue, was enraged that justice was not done and did not want to wait for another trial. Grace, Lieutenant Thomas Massie, and two navy-enlisted men kidnapped Joseph Kahahawai, who was one of the five charged suspects, and attempted to get him to confess to raping Thalia. In roughing up Kahahawai, one in the group of four shot and killed him.

On January 8, 1932, Grace, Thomas, and the two navy men were arrested for kidnapping and killing Kahahawai. When the grand jury indicted the four suspects on the charge of second-degree murder, they contacted Darrow to defend them. When Darrow became acquainted with the case, he realized that there was no doubt that the four defendants caused Kahahawai's death, and he began to think what extenuating circumstances would be most helpful to get an acquittal from the jury ("Massie Trial," *Wikipedia*).

Some of Darrow's Closing Comments

There is somewhere deep in the feelings and instincts of a man, a yearning for justice, an idea of what is right and wrong, of what is fair between man and man, that came before the first law was written and will abide after the last one is dead. If you put yourself in Tommie Massie's place, what would you have done? (Farrell n.d.)

If you want to send [Grace] to the penitentiary, all right, go to it. If this wife and mother, this husband and these faithful boys go to the penitentiary, it won't be the first time the penitentiary has been sanctified by its inmates. It won't be the first time the name of the jail will be remembered when every jailer has been forgotten. When people come here, the first thing they will wish to see is where the mother and husband are confined. If it should happen, that building will be the most conspicuous building on this island and people will wonder at the cruelty and injustice of man. (Lindner 2007)

The Verdict

On April 29, 1932, the jury returned with a verdict of manslaughter and recommended leniency. One week later, Judge Charles Skinner Davis sentenced the defendants to ten years hard labor—the mandatory sentence for manslaughter in Hawaii.

Governor Lawrence Judd, who had the power to pardon the defendants, thought carefully about his decision. At the same time, important naval personnel and powerful leaders in the states were demanding a full pardon for all the defendants. The defense attorneys who were in Judd's office at the time said that the governor received a telephone call from President Herbert Hoover, who urged that all four should not receive any jail time (Lindner 2007).

Several days later, Governor Judd commuted their sentences to one hour in his office. About a week later, Lieutenant Massie, Thalia, and her mother left for San Francisco. There never was a retrial for the group of five, which Thalia claimed assaulted her. Three decades later, Deacon Jones, one of the navy-enlisted men in the group of four suspects, admitted that he fired the shot that killed Joseph Kahahawai.

Darrow, the great defender of the underdog, chose the other side here. Although everyone deserves an attorney, Darrow's participation in this case was both sad and disappointing.

Bombing: *Los Angeles Times*

We now return to the Bombing of the *Los Angeles Times* building. Harrison Gray Otis, who owned the *Los Angeles Times*, played an important role in keeping the trade unions out of Los Angeles. On October 1, 1910, members of the International Association of Bridge and Structural Iron Workers (Iron Workers) went on strike demanding an increase in wages. Otis and the Merchants and Manufacturers Association, however, managed to break the strike. Shortly after 1:00 a.m. on October 1, 1910, the *Los Angeles Times* building was bombed; the explosion and fire caused twenty-one deaths and injured one hundred more. The explosion was so violent that many panic-stricken people from blocks around thought that an enormous earthquake had hit the city. For that time, it was comparable to the destruction of the World Trade Center in 2001.

The police investigators learned that James B. McNamara and Ortie McManigal were possible suspects in the bombing. In April 1911 they were arrested for a bank robbery. When questioned later, McManigal turned state's evidence and told the police about the bombing of the *Los Angeles Times* building, implicating James B. McNamara, his brother John J. McNamara, and himself. On April 26, all three were taken into custody and transported from Chicago to Los Angeles. Then on May 5, the McNamara bothers were arraigned and pled not guilty; however, McManigal was not charged at the time.

Events Leading to the Trial

Frank Ryan, president of the Iron Workers, sought out Darrow to defend the McNamara brothers. On May 1911, Darrow left Chicago and arrived in Los Angeles to join the defense team and agreed to be the lead defense attorney. Prior to the time that the jury was seated, Darrow became increasingly concerned that the prosecution had a very strong case, so he began to work out a plea agreement to save the defendants' lives. He was able to convince the McNamaras that a settlement was possible if they both pled guilty.

Meanwhile, District Attorney John D. Fredericks got wind that Bert Franklin, the defense team's chief investigator, had contacted two jurors with a bribe offer and vote to acquit the McNamaras. On November 28, 1911, just three days prior to the trial, Fredericks had arranged a "sting" operation and arrested Franklin after he handed over the bribe money to one of the jurors. Darrow, who had hurried to the bribe scene after receiving a telephone call in his office, was just a short distance away and saw what happened. But why would Darrow be in the immediate vicinity of the illegal transaction?

When Darrow was accused of jury tampering on November 28, the defense's hope for a simple plea agreement ended. On December 1, the McNamara brothers now pled guilty in open court. James B. McNamara, who admitted to setting off the explosion, was sentenced to life imprisonment, while John J. McNamara was sentenced to fifteen years in prison.

Darrow on Trial—Enter Earl Rogers

In January 1912, Franklin pled guilty to charges of jury tampering and shortly afterward testified that he was acting on orders from Darrow, who had planned the bribery of the two jurors.

District Attorney Fredericks obtained two indictments against Darrow, one for each juror: each count to be tried separately. Darrow immediately contacted Earl Rogers to lead his defense team.

Rogers was one of the most famous criminal lawyers of his time. His reputation was such that if anyone were accused of a crime they would say, "Get me Earl Rogers." He appeared for the defense in seventy-seven murder trials and only lost three.

Earl Rogers: Hall of Fame Lawyer

Earl Rogers

Rogers was considered to be a "technological" pioneer in his day. It was a time when there was no television, there was little radio, and most of what was going on in the world came out in newspapers. He was the first attorney to effectively use all kinds of visual aids in the courtroom: blackboards, charts, and blow-ups to make his point.

Rogers presented the evidence in a revolutionary way to the jurors so they could more easily understand the issues. He believed that while preparation was important, it was mandatory to have the proper presentation to reach the jury. He was clever in maneuvering and seducing juries with his histrionics, and he had a flair for theatrically.

On one occasion, he brought the intestines of the victim into the court to show that his client was lying down while the victim was hovering over him when he was forced to shoot in self-defense. On another occasion, Rogers had his client take a seat in the spectator's section and moved another person to sit next to him at the counsel table. His client was acquitted when the victim identified the wrong person.

He often used a technique through which he re-created the crime scene in the courtroom: the poker-table case is an example. The prosecution's eyewitness stated that Roger's client shot the victim while they were all seated at a poker table. The witness said that he just sat there at the table during the shooting. Rogers then introduced a poker table into evidence and sat down with the witness at the card table. Suddenly Rogers pulled out a revolver from his coat and pointed it to the witness who reacted quickly and shouted and fell backward. He was able to show that the eyewitness was lying and his client was acquitted.

On one occasion he employed a fencing expert to illustrate how his client, who shot a well-known attorney, was parrying the victim's attack with nothing but a cane.

In some cases he would carry out the scene by himself to demonstrate a critical point or even employ an expert to re-create the event right in front of the jury. He was often able to show witnesses inconsistencies using this method. Once a witness stated that the accused presented a pocket gold watch in his right hand as collateral in a wager. When the offer was turned down, he "quick as lightning" pulled out a revolver from his pocket and shot the other person. Rogers then handed the witness a gold watch from his pocket and then handed him the revolver in evidence and asked him to show the jury how he could hold the watch in his hand and "in lightning speed" produce a revolver in the same hand to shoot the victim. When the witness did an about face, Rogers's client was acquitted ("Great Trial Lawyers from the Past—Earl Rogers" 2007).

Rogers was an avid reader and became adept in using forensics and won a number of cases through his skillful cross-examinations of medical experts presented by the prosecution. He was also the first attorney to introduce the science of ballistics into a criminal trial. In one case, Rogers was defending three California police officers who were accused of shooting down two men in cold blood: the officers claimed self-defense. The case was well publicized, and the public generally believed the police would be found guilty. Rogers brought in experts along with photos of the bullets taken from the crime scene. He was able to show that the victims fired at the three police officers and that certain bullets found at the crime scene did not match the officers' weapons. The result: the case was dismissed.

He was also the first lawyer to successfully defend an important murder case on grounds of "alcoholic insanity." (A sad first for Rogers, as we shall see.) He brought a psychiatrist into the courtroom to testify and prove that alcohol can have a lasting effect on the nervous system and brain.

In one of his most celebrated cases, his client Colonel Griffith J. Griffith, a Welsh-American industrialist and philanthropist, accused his young wife of infidelities. While in a rage of drunken jealousy, he forced his wife down to her knees to confess her wrongdoing while he held a gun close to her temple. The defense maintained that she moved her head when he fired and shot out one of her eyes. Tragically, it turned out that she was not guilty of any indiscretions.

The judge, however, sentenced Griffith to only two years in San Quentin State Prison. He also gave instructions that Griffith should be given "medical aid for his condition of alcoholic insanity."

Rogers would always ask the "how" and "why" questions in cross-examinations and, in doing so, would often break down the prosecution's expert witnesses. He always attempted to put another person on trial rather than his own client. Depending on the situation, he would choose the victim, or an eyewitness, or a police officer—anyone else other than the defendant.

According to Rogers's daughter, Adela, he had a penchant for "second sight, sixth sense…and psychic conclusions arrived at by convolutions of the soul and the stomach, as well as the brain" (Mesereau 2006).

Rogers was not satisfied to live in a world of a privileged few and just enjoy his successes. He had a passion for helping the downtrodden. It was said that he had many friends—from police officers to others in the red-light district downtown.

He was very fashionable and always well dressed. At different times, he would wear satin waistcoats, patent leather shoes, spats, a flashy Cravat, and diamond-studded pearl stickpins—and he always wore a gardenia in his buttonhole. He was even known to change suits over the noon hour, and he always "fiddled" with his gold lorgnette.

Rogers enjoyed spending money and he liked to drink. He could not control his drinking, and eventually he sank into a drunken state of irresponsibility. His son finally signed a complaint to have him committed; Adela also appeared in court against him. After her testimony ended, Rogers approached her slowly at the witness box and asked her softly, "You don't think I'm crazy, do you, honey?" Adela, who had wanted her father committed for his own well-being, broke down under Rogers's last great cross-examination and said, "No." Rogers was not committed. Soon afterward, he died an alcoholic and broke, living in a flophouse in Los Angeles: he was fifty-two years old (Smith 1989).

If you want to read more about Earl Rogers, we recommend a wonderful book titled *Final Verdict* by his daughter, Adela Rogers St. Johns.

Adela Rogers St. Johns

Darrow on Trial

We now return to the street scene and the beginning of this story when Bert Franklin was arrested for attempting to bribe a juror, and Darrow was close by watching it all happen. In January 1912, Franklin pled guilty, but then he told the authorities that Darrow had planned the jury-tampering operation.

Prior to the trial, Darrow often disagreed with Rogers on how his case should be handled. According to Adela Rogers St. Johns, her father spent an inordinate amount of time trying to convince Darrow and his wife to accept his views on how the case should be tried.

> [We] had an almost daily row over Darrow's courtroom behavior and continual scraps about the three lines of defense and which came first so that a lot of the time my father was as restless as a .400 hitter benched in the World Series. The drive it took my father to control Darrow's desire and insistence that the defense rest entirely on the conspiracy-frame-up basis was mounting into hot or icy quarrels. On several occasions Rogers threatened to quit him flat if he persisted in some course that Earl believed was wrong. ("Earl Rogers," *Wikipedia*)

Rogers was finally able to get Darrow not to make the argument to essentially condone the dynamiting of the *Los Angeles Times* building and also killing all those innocent people. Rogers's summary was curt and to the point, stating that Darrow was too intelligent to get involved in a bribery scheme and that he certainly would not have knowingly run up the street to the bribery scene, calling attention to himself.

Darrow specifically drew attention to a witness for the prosecution who said that Darrow rushed across the street waving his hat. In a typical fashion, Rogers stepped off to one side of the courtroom and took his own stylish hat off from the rack and began to wave it wildly while prancing in front of the jury. He was re-creating the "alleged scene" for all to see—especially the jurors. The reenactment was to show the jury how unbelievable that would be if someone were guilty.

On August 15, 1912, Darrow was acquitted after the jury deliberated for less than an hour.

Darrow on Trial—the Second Charge

In November 1912, Darrow was put on trial for an alleged bribery of the second juror. While Rogers began this trial as the lead attorney, he became ill and rarely returned to court. It was generally conceded that if Rogers was leading the second trial, he would have been successful in getting a second acquittal for Darrow.

Darrow, however, was now free to defend himself. He attempted to condone the purposeful dynamiting of the *Los Angeles Times* building and the resulting death of twenty-one people as a social crime rather than a horrendous killing. Darrow went on for some time admitting to some of his failings. In his famous closing argument, he promised to be a better person and that he had learned his lesson.

The jury was unable to reach a unanimous decision, since only eight of the twelve jurors thought Darrow was guilty. It was a hung jury and they were dismissed.

The prosecution team decided to drop any attempt for a third trial if Darrow agreed not to practice law in California. Darrow then returned to Chicago disgraced, where he continued to practice law with little money in his pocket. After several years, he managed to revive his reputation as a criminal lawyer and again become the "Attorney for the Damned." He became the focus of public-media attention in 1924 when he defended the Leopold and Loeb thrill-killers and also in the following year as the hero in the Scopes trial. He died on March 13, 1938, at age eighty-one. He requested that his ashes be scattered over a bridge in Chicago's Jackson Park ("Earl Rogers," *Wikipedia*).

Darrow's Downfall

So what are we to think—was Darrow guilty or not?

When Darrow began his career, he soon earned a reputation as a defender of the downtrodden. Later, however, he spent much of his professional time working for clients who paid him well. He received a retainer of $50,000 (equivalent to about $1.2 million in 2016) from the America Federation of Labor (AFL) in the McNamara case. After Darrow pointed out that he needed $350,000 (equivalent to about $8.9 million in 2016) for the defense, the AFL quickly began to raise additional funds ("*Los Angeles Times* Bombing," *Wikipedia*).

When Darrow took the stand in his own defense, he pleaded not guilty in both trials. He also stated that Franklin's testimony against him was a downright lie. Darrow, however, did not say that he was innocent but told that his conscience was clear—he differentiated between moral and legal guilt (Farrell 2011).

In his second trial he was bold and gave a memorable closing argument—suggesting that the McNamara bothers were justified for their terrorist action because the rich and powerful were exploiting the common workers. Darrow went on to say:

He had seen their flesh and blood ground into money for the rich. He had seen the little children working in factories and mills; he has seen death in every form coming from the oppression of the strong and the powerful; and he struck out blindly in the dark to do what he thought would help...I shall always be thankful that I had the courage to represent him [Jim McNamara]. (Farrell 2011)

After hearing Darrow's final poignant remarks, jurors told reporters they felt that Darrow would indeed resort to bribery to defend and support his own views and those of his clients.

While some early biographers concluded that it was likely Darrow was innocent, Attorney Geoffrey Cowan, who studied the first trial in detail, believed that he was guilty.

Mary Fields, who was a journalist and Darrow's mistress, always maintained that he was innocent. But author John A. Farrell, in his book *Clarence Darrow: Attorney for the Damned*, found a notation in Field's diary that ended with "If men are so cruel as to break other men's necks, so greedy as to be restrained only by money, then a sensitive man must bribe to save."

In searching Darrow's long-lost letters, Farrell wrote, "And there I found a 1927 letter from Darrow to his son, Paul, instructing him to pay $4500" (equivalent to about $56,000 in 2016) to Fred Golding, a juror in the first bribery trial. It's of interest to note that Golding was Darrow's most strident defender on the jury (Farrell 2011).

Leo Cherne, the philanthropist, came into possession of some of Darrow's papers from 1911 to 1912. One telegram that Darrow sent to his brother Everett on the day he was indicted read as follows: "Can't make myself feel guilty. My conscience refuses to reproach me."

Farrell also wrote that neither he nor Attorney Cowan "found evidence of a conspiracy to frame Darrow in the files of the U. S. Justice Department, or in the papers of Walter Drew, the steel industry's union-busting lobbyist, who had led and helped fund the case against the McNamaras" (Farrell 2011).

Adela Rogers St. Johns wrote in *Final Verdict*:

I really suffered during the Darrow trial. If they pulled out my toenails, I would still know we had to get Darrow off. He was our client. Right or wrong I was for Papa, but for the first time I wasn't clearhearted rip-roaring all the way out, every once in a while I'd find myself drifting to the other side unconsciously. I knew he was guilty, and I couldn't seem to justify it.

Adela also wrote:

Perhaps, with Papa, it was when he knew Darrow was guilty or when the district attorney roused Darrow out of town and told him never to try to practice law in California again and Darrow went without saying good-by—or thank you.

So how should we judge Darrow? While Darrow was a great orator and legendary figure, the evidence suggests that he did indeed resort to bribery. We think he was guilty as hell of the charge. Whether you think he was, nevertheless, still on the side of the angels will depend on your own political views.

(The outcome of the trials and the union-backed violence practically crippled the labor movement until FDR's New Deal in the 1930s.)

Lost in the Amazon—Hunting for Z

As Percy Fawcett fought his way into the Brazilian jungle in his search for the Lost City of Z, he encountered suffocating heat and hordes of deadly mosquitoes, venomous snakes, shrunken human heads, and hostile Indians with poison arrows. But Fawcett, the last great flamboyant explorer of the twentieth century, was fearless as he journeyed deeper and deeper into uncharted territories of the dark tropical forest.

The Amazon, however, was a deathtrap like no other, since it has led many other explorers before him to starvation, madness, death, and disappearances. While Fawcett was able to endure inconceivable hardships better than anyone, there were other hidden mysteries and horrendous hazards lying beneath the impenetrable massive jungle canopy of the Amazon. The legendary explorer, however, was obsessed to find Z, the city of gold, even though his quest was filled with exotic and unknown dangers.

It's 1925, and Calvin Coolidge, the thirtieth president of the United States, became the first president to have his inaugural ceremony broadcast nationally on radio. Federal spending is $2.9 billion and unemployment is only 2.3 percent. Nellie Tayloe Ross takes office as governor of Wyoming: she is the first woman governor in US history. George Bernard Shaw is awarded the Nobel Prize for literature, and John T. Scopes is arrested for teaching evolution in Tennessee, which is the first state to outlaw teaching the theory of evolution.

And in 1925, Fawcett headed off with his son, Jack, and Jack's best friend, Raleigh, on his final expedition to search for a vanished city, never to be heard from again. What happened to them? Was it Fawcett's destiny to be drawn and lured into the jungle's "green hell"? His disappearance has been an unsolved riddle for over ninety years. But then, it's always possible that his murky fate might someday come to light.

Background

Percy Fawcett was born on August 18, 1867, in Devon, England. He was educated in Britain's elite public schools, including the Newton School, Newton Abbott, and Westminster.

In 1884, at the age of seventeen, he was sent off to the Royal Military Academy at Woolwich. Two years later, he received a commission and was assigned to the British colony of Ceylon (now Sri Lanka). He served for several years in Ceylon, where he met his wife, Nina Patterson. They had two sons, Jack and Brian.

Fawcett was a sturdy well-built man, over six feet tall, and had a reputation for being fearless. He sported an impressive military-style moustache and had piercing steel blue eyes. He was gritty, tough, and eccentric.

In 1901, He joined the Royal Geographic Society (RGS), where he studied mapmaking and surveying. Later, he went on to work for the British Secret Service in North Africa. Fawcett, however, became bored with army life and was seeking something more adventuresome, so he returned to England in 1902.

In early 1906, the president of the RGS pointed out all the blank spaces on a map of South America to Fawcett and the critical need for more reliable maps. The president also spoke of the need to establish better-defined borders between the various countries. Finally, he called attention to the huge economic potential of South America and asked Fawcett if he was interested in doing some surveying and mapmaking in that remote and dangerous region of the world on behalf of the RGS. The offer was just what Fawcett was looking for: it was his ticket to adventure.

Early Expeditions

In 1906, at the age of thirty-nine, Fawcett started on his first expedition to South America. After arriving in La Plaz, the capital of Bolivia, in

June of that year, he quickly got started off on his journey into the heart of the jungle to begin his boundary survey work.

Fawcett began his journey by leading a small exploratory group, including natives and pack mules, into the Amazon. He soon realized that it would be difficult just to get to the area where he would begin his work. His assignment was to map an area between Bolivia and Brazil; however, the two countries were feuding over the boundaries between their native lands. Fawcett was sent to the region as a fair-minded referee whose decisions could be trusted.

There were untold hazards—fording raging rivers, facing vicious piranhas, dodging deadly snakes, warding off hordes of wicked insects, dealing with giant electric eels, and encountering various diseases—it wasn't for the faint-hearted. Furthermore, it was a lawless territory, much like the early American West.

While on this expedition in 1907, Fawcett claimed to have seen a giant Anaconda that was longer than sixty feet. At that length, it could weigh about one thousand pounds and even swallow a whole deer. (Fawcett, however, was known to have a lively imagination. It is fair to say that if we both were along with Fawcett at that time, it would have been our last expedition.) The largest Anaconda ever measured was about twenty-eight feet long with a girth of forty-four inches: and that's awesome.

Percy Fawcett

Fawcett was outraged by how poorly the plantation owners treated the South American Indians. The owners often sent parties into the jungle to capture natives and then overwork them. Some tribes, however, started to turn hostile toward outsiders because of how poorly they were treated. Fawcett believed that if he dealt with the natives in a civil manner, they would be understanding and friendly. He was proud of how well he got along with the natives and always presented them with gifts.

In his 1908 expedition, Fawcett found the source of the Rio Verde River in Brazil. Then, in the 1910 expedition, he followed the Heath River, which is between Bolivia and Peru, and also located its source.

Discovering the source of any river is a significant accomplishment, and finding the source of a major river is a remarkable achievement. (The source of the Nile River, the longest in the world, baffled explorers for thousands of years. As early as 66 CE, the Emperor Nero directed an expedition to find the legendary headwaters of the Nile. But it wasn't until the fall of 1858 that John Hanning Speke first reached Lake Victoria in the heart of Africa and then returned to establish it as the source of the Nile in 1862.)

The mighty Amazon River, which is the largest river by discharge of water in the world, was discovered only about five hundred years ago. Its source, however, has been a controversy for centuries. As recent as 1971, a National Geographic expedition reported finding the source of the Amazon, but in 2000 a National Geographic team reported that they found another source. A recent research team using GPS tracking data and satellite imagery has reported still another new source, which might show that the Amazon is also the longest river in the world. The matter, however, does not appear to be completely settled since they're debating the issue of whether the source is continuous or interrupted.

Fawcett's expedition teams all faced extreme difficulties and deadly hazards. They not only had to cut their way through the dense jungle but also trekked along makeshift trails and up precipitous paths in the mountains at fifteen thousand feet. The pack mules, while critical to their success, could not be overworked: losing a mule was akin to losing a man. In many instances, they had to build their own canoes from trees at hand, in order to navigate some of the swift-flowing rivers.

Furthermore, not everyone in an expedition party returned alive. Fawcett almost lost his life on several occasions. He was, however, a tough, fearless explorer. Once Fawcett and his party were warned not to travel up the Heath River, since tribes along the way had a reputation for indiscriminate savagery. An army major said, "To venture up into the midst of them is sheer madness." And what did Fawcett do?—he went anyway (Grann 2009).

The Outbreak of World War I

Fawcett made six expeditions from 1906 through 1914. When he returned from some of his adventures, scientists and many other notables, including Sir Arthur Conan Doyle, would attend the RGS hall to hear him speak. Fawcett became friends with the famous author and also corresponded with him. Doyle had also drawn on Fawcett's field-trip reports for his 1912 novel *The Lost World*.

The idea of the Lost City of Z came to Fawcett over a period of time. It began while he was serving in the military in Ceylon. He drew up his thoughts of Z more clearly while on an expedition in Brazil in 1914 and was convinced that Z was located somewhere in the heart of the jungle. After a yearlong expedition in the fall of that year, he planned to finally begin his search for the City of Gold. Shortly after returning from the jungle, however, he learned that World War I had begun: he immediately made arrangements to return to England.

When Fawcett arrived in England, he had a short visit with his family and was soon sent off to the Western Front; he was now a major in the Royal Field Artillery. He volunteered for active duty in Flanders and was in command of an artillery brigade of over seven hundred men. Fawcett, who was accustomed to inhuman conditions, adapted well to the harsh trench warfare and was respected by those who served under his command. In 1916, as he was approaching fifty years of age, he was promoted to lieutenant colonel.

Fawcett and his troops participated in The Battle of the Somme, which started on July 1, 1916, and lasted until November 18, of that year.

The casualty figures were appalling on all sides. At the end of the battle, the British Army had suffered 420,000 casualties, including 60,000 on the very first day! That first day was the bloodiest twenty-four hours in the history of the British Army. The French lost 200,000 soldiers, and the Germans lost nearly 500,000.

Fawcett was awarded the Distinguished Service Order medal on January 4, 1917, for his bravery. The war then dragged on for almost another two years and finally ended on November 11, 1918.

The Postwar Years

Fawcett then returned to his home in England. It was the first time in years that he saw his wife and children. Jack, the oldest son, was now sixteen years of age; he was strong and powerful like his father and filled with his father's sense of adventure.

For ten long years prior to the war while Fawcett had explored the remote jungle, he was constantly searching for clues that would lead him closer to The Lost City of Z. He was convinced that he knew where it was and that he would eventually find it. And now his mission was to begin to plan other expeditions to the Amazon: he would not be denied.

Fawcett was disappointed when the RGS and other institutions turned down his requests to fund future explorations. In January 1920, he moved his family to Jamaica. One month later, he sailed off to South America, seeking funding from the Brazilian government for future expeditions.

He managed to obtain sufficient funds for two short undertakings to the Amazon, but they did not turn out well. In the fall of 1921, he was forced to return from his second short and disastrous journey into the jungle. Nevertheless, Fawcett vowed that he would return. The next several years, however, were disappointing since he had little success in raising funds.

Fawcett's Rival

During most of the years Fawcett had been exploring the Amazon, he had a rival named Alexander Hamilton Rice, who was a surgeon and an explorer. (His wife, philanthropist Eleanor Elkins Weidner, donated the funds to Harvard University for Widener Library as a memorial to her son after his death in the sinking of the *Titanic*.) Rice's vast resources gave him a distinct advantage over Fawcett, who always feared that Rice would discover Z first.

Rice could easily afford to purchase the latest equipment as well as employ highly skilled men for his large expeditions. He had a forty-five-foot powered boat, bulky radar equipment, and the latest communication equipment, which allowed him to communicate with newspapers and radio stations while wandering through the jungle. He even had a hydroplane, which was equipped with aerial cameras. Fawcett, however, felt that it would be difficult to penetrate the jungle canopy by aerial observation and photography; and carrying all that bulky equipment has its limitations in the Amazon. Was he right, or was it just sour grapes?

In a 1920 expedition, Rice and his party encountered the Yanomami tribe, who were known as "white Indians" because of their light-colored skin. While he offered them gifts, the Yanomami not only refused the gifts but also confronted the explorers. When Rice gave the order to fire a warning shot over their heads, the Indians began to unleash their arrows at the intruders. In turn, his men opened fire and killed an untold number of Yanomami. Later, Rice communicated to the RGS that he had no choice but to defend themselves. Fawcett, on the other hand, was outraged and vehemently spoke out against the use of such tactics.

In a later expedition, *The New York Times* reported in one of its articles that Rice's hydroplane carried "some bombs," which were to be used to frighten the native Indians. Fawcett, of course, was also appalled at such horrific action. Being bombed from the sky could hardly have made the natives happier; clearly, intrusive visitors were not welcome—as Fawcett may have sadly learned later.

Nevertheless, Fawcett and Rice were each awarded a gold medal by the RGS for the meritorious work that they carried out on their jungle expeditions.

Contrast in Searching Techniques

The contrast between Percy Fawcett and Dr. Alexander Hamilton Rice was significant: it was a case of have and have-not. Fawcett was a colorful, adventurous swashbuckler who ventured into the Amazon on foot with sheer determination and toughness. He was a true explorer who relied on his grit and cunning in his battle with the hostile environment. He was the last great individualist explorer of the twentieth century: he did much to chart parts of South America, which prior to him were simply blank spaces on a map.

Fawcett was like those other British explorers a generation before him. In the late 1860s, missionary David Livingstone, who set out on foot searching for the source of the Nile, disappeared in the heart of Africa. About a decade later in 1871, Henry Stanley journeyed into the Dark Continent, vowing to find him. Unbelievably, ten months later, Stanley not only found him but gained immortality with his famous greeting: "Dr. Livingstone, I presume?" (According to Tim Jeal, author of *Explorers of the Nile: The Triumph and Tragedy of a Great Victoria Adventure*, that famous phrase does not seem to be Stanley's first comment when he met Dr. Livingstone. But whatever it was that Stanley first said appears to be lost to history.)

Rice, on the other hand, explored the Amazon with a large party and the best and most expensive technology to carry out his missions. He did, however, show the way, but it would be another ten years before his exploratory methods using modern technology would be accepted. Today we see highly trained research teams with the latest scientific equipment carrying out research in remote and hazardous environments such as the Antarctic and outer space.

The Final Expedition

By 1924, Fawcett managed to obtain financial backing from a variety of sources for his return to the Amazon. He was fifty-seven years of age, and this was his last chance to find Z. Finally, on December 3 of that year, the road to Z seemed to be secure. Fawcett and his oldest son,

Jack, said good-bye to their family and boarded the *Aquitania* bound for New York, where Raleigh Rimell, Jack's best friend, would join them on the expedition. Upon their arrival in the United States, Fawcett learned that one of his financial backers was no longer able to support him. Fortunately, John D. Rockefeller Jr., the billionaire, contributed sufficient finds, which enabled Fawcett to quickly move forward and embark on the journey to the jungle.

By late January 1925, Fawcett, Jack, and Raleigh were in Rio de Janeiro. The two young men were strong, sturdy, and also adventurous; they were also eager and excited to be part of the trek to find Z. On February 11, they left Rio and traveled by train and boat to Corumba. On February 23, they loaded all their equipment on board the *Iquatemi*, a small dirty boat, and headed north to Cuiaba, Brazil, which was the capital of Mato Grosso, (thick forest) located along the southern part of the Amazon basin. They had finally reached their point of departure on their 1,000-mile journey into the jungle of Brazil.

Jack Fawcett and Raleigh Rimell

Fawcett always preferred small expeditions, and this one was no exception. They packed food items, flares, guns, a sextant, and a chronometer to determine latitude and longitude and an aneroid barometer for measuring atmospheric pressure. He also carried a small glycerin compass in his pocket. Fawcett took along two native guides, four horses, eight donkeys, and two dogs. He felt that a small exploratory party would be able to live off the land and in general progress faster with less difficulty than a much larger group. Also, a small party would appear less threatening to the native Indians.

On April 25, Fawcett led his small expedition from Cuiaba: at long last, they were off. By evening of that day, they traveled seven miles and he decided to set up camp. Before dawn the next day, they were off again, and soon Fawcett increased their daily junkets to ten and then to fifteen miles. The insects were horrible, the weather was hot, and it rained often; the food was plain but sustained them. At one point, Fawcett raced ahead and the others in the party lost sight of him. Jack and Raleigh, who were tough and adventurous, were pleased to see him the next day when he showed up.

By May 16, they arrived at Bakairi Post after traveling approximately 150 miles. Traveling was becoming more difficult, especially when they had to cross over rivers, and also to contend with dangerous rapids. At Bakairi, they saw eight wild Indians (five men, two women, and a child) completely naked who came to the post from the nearby Xingu region. They carried long bows and arrows and stood about five feet two inches in height and were strong and hardy.

On May 17, the small Fawcett party sat around a fire that night. Fawcett tool out his ukulele, Jack got his piccolo, and that was the evening concert. Raleigh was selected to take pictures, including, of course, those Indians without clothes.

On May 19, they celebrated Jack's twenty-second birthday. The three men made merry with a bottle of Brazilian-made liquor.

On May 20, they prepared their equipment along with the pack mules; it was time to move on. The following day the party started north, and now they were headed into unexplored jungle territory as well as facing imposing mountains ahead. There was no clear path to follow, and only a little light from the blazing sun was able to penetrate through the canopy.

Traveling continued to become even more difficult; they had to use machetes to cut their way through the thick jungle. The ever-present mosquitoes took more than their fair share of blood as they trekked their way to a place called Dead Horse Camp.

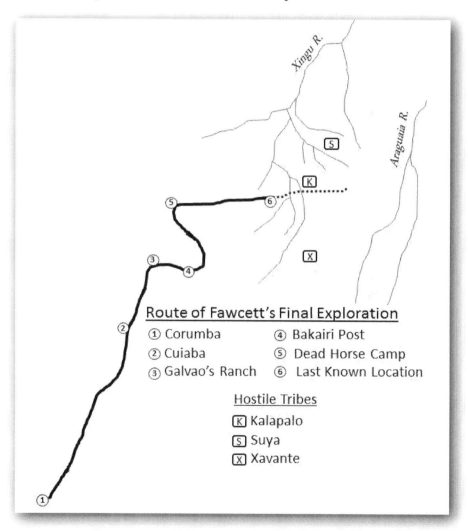

Route of Fawcett's Final Exploration

① Corumba   ④ Bakairi Post

② Cuiaba   ⑤ Dead Horse Camp

③ Galvao's Ranch   ⑥ Last Known Location

Hostile Tribes

Ⓚ Kalapalo

Ⓢ Suya

Ⓧ Xavante

On May 29, after nine brutal days, they finally fought their way to Dead Horse Camp, about one hundred miles from Bakairi Post. At this point, the two native guides decided that they did not want to go on any farther. Fawcett tried to encourage Raleigh, who had more than his share of difficulty on the expedition to date, to also return with the guides. Raleigh, however, chose to stay with party. Fawcett selected several strong animals to stay with them for several more days, after which the three men would have to carry all their own provisions.

On that late day in May, Fawcett wrote his final letter to his wife telling her that they are at Dead Horse Camp. He mentioned that it was the same location where his horse died in his expedition in 1921, but now, only his white bones remain. Fawcett designated the location as latitude 11 degrees 43' South and longitude 54 degrees 35' West. His last words to his wife were, "You need have no fear of any failure."

In a report to the North American Newspapers Alliance (NANA), Fawcett reported that the latitude was 13 degrees 43' South and longitude as 54 degrees 35' West: this location was 140 miles directly north of Dead Horse Camp. He either made a mistake or more likely intentionally reported the incorrect latitude for the purpose of misleading others who might try to follow his trail.

Fawcett, Jack, and Raleigh gave a farewell wave to the small group of Brazilians at the camp, as they turned and headed northeast to the Xingu River. They were apparently planning to cross the Upper Xingu, which is a 1,230-mile-long tributary of the Amazon River and then head north into the forest between the Xingu River and the Araguaia River.

Then, somewhere along the way, they vanished—never to be seen or heard from again (Grann 2009).

Searching for Fawcett

Percy Fawcett's disappearance is one of the great jungle-exploration mysteries of the twentieth century. The Fawcett expedition did not plan to return until 1927; however, when they never made it back, the newspapers began speculating on what might have happened to them. The stories quickly got the public's attention and fascinated readers. While Fawcett stated that no one should start looking for them if they failed to return, more than thirteen search parties have attempted to discover what happened to him and his two companions. Not only have they all failed but also about one hundred people eventually died trying to determine their fate.

Numerous rumors and unverified reports have circulated for years concerning Fawcett's disappearance. From time to time researchers have reported finding his compass, nameplate, and even his bones—but none of the findings have ever been confirmed.

Fawcett even had an influence on popular culture, and a number of books have been written about his fate. A Russian documentary film has been released about his final expedition, and a film of his life by Paramount Pictures was made. As we noted earlier, Sir Arthur Conan Doyle based the character Professor Challenger, in part, on Fawcett. Stories of *The Lost City of Z* were the basis for his book titled *The Lost World*. Director Peter Docter used Fawcett as his inspiration for Charles F. Muntz, the rival of the Pixar Jones, the fictional adventurer film *Up*. It has even been suggested that Fawcett was the model for Indiana Jones, the fictional adventurer.

In 1996, over seven decades after Fawcett disappeared, Rene Delmotte and James Lynch headed up an expedition to look for evidence of what might have happened to him. Even this recent attempt shows how dangerous it can be to venture into those unchartered territories of the Amazon—the expedition didn't progress very far before they were stopped by native Indians. The search team was threatened and also detained for a period of time. Eventually, they were released, but only after $30,000 worth of equipment was confiscated.

Even after decades, danger continues to lurk in the mysterious Amazon, where Fawcett, Jack, and Raleigh were last known to be—and woe to those who attempt to follow in their footsteps. Their fate remains a haunting mystery to this day ("Percy Fawcett," *Wikipedia*).

Fawcett's Fate

So really what happened to Fawcett, Jack, and Raleigh? While Fawcett had survived many dangers on numerous other expeditions, why did he never return?

Did they encounter jaguars, Piranhas, or some other vicious creatures that ended their journey? While the dangerous jungle animals always pose a threat, the men had guns and were good shooters, so we feel that it is not likely they met their death in this manner.

Did the three men contact some disease that resulted in their demise? While they were probably sick at different times, we do not think that in their final days all three succumbed to some deadly disease.

When the trio left Dead Horse Camp, they were tired, weary, and not in top physical shape, but they went on. They were, however, headed into territories where there were known to be various hostile Indian tribes. After a few days they would have to start carrying their own provisions, which now made their travel through the dense forest even more difficult. It's possible that a combination of illness and injury slowed them down significantly, and also their food wasn't sufficient to sustain them. Raleigh, in particular, was having difficulty, and it's almost impossible to carry someone very far in the middle of the jungle. Furthermore, they were not physically fit enough to forage for food, and their health deteriorated to the point where they might have died of starvation. We think this scenario is more likely than the previous two.

At some point in their trek through the jungle, they not only were encountering more hostile tribes but were now completely surrounded by the hostile Kalapalos, Suyas, and Xavants, as shown on the route map.

The Kalapalos Indians

The three men were weary, ill, and hardly able to carry on. We think that they were easily subdued and captured by one of the hostile tribes. The haggard explorers were helpless: furthermore, they did not have any gifts to present to the natives who expected gifts. We think they were viewed as enemy intruders by some unknown hostile tribe and murdered.

If Fawcett had his choice, we think he would have preferred to have mysteriously disappeared in the Amazon, with his indomitable spirit living on rather than returning without finding Z, and no doubt viewing himself as a failure. And, in his own inimitable way, he did not fail his rendezvous with death. (We're less confident that Jack and, especially, Raleigh felt exactly the same way.)

Aftermath

Author Evan Andrews wrote the following regarding journalist David Grann's journey in 2005 to retrace Fawcett's last trek through the Amazon.

> During a meeting with Kalapalo Indians, he [Grann] learned that the tribe had preserved the tale of a meeting with the explorer in their oral history. The Indians claimed Fawcett had disregarded their warnings and trekked into the domain of a warlike tribe the Kalapalos called the "fierce Indians." When the white men failed to return, the Kalapalos concluded that they had been ambushed and killed. (Andrews n.d.)

A Fanciful Tale

There is yet another explanation, which is fanciful, that bears mentioning. By the time they reached the Xingu River, Raleigh had become seriously ill and died. Fawcett and Jack were totally exhausted, their food supply had run out, and they were unable to continue on. Sometime later, an Indian tribe found the two men but they were near death.

Somehow, using primitive jungle medicines, they were able to keep Fawcett alive: Jack, who had sacrificed his own health in trying to save Raleigh, also died.

After many weeks of raving and ranting, Fawcett managed to wake up, but he could not remember anything: he had total memory loss. The Indian tribe took Fawcett to be their new chief and leader. All Fawcett knew was his immediate surroundings and could not relate to anything else.

He went on to live the rest of his life peacefully and happily as the new leader of the tribe. Wasn't it, after all, in his subconscious mind that he would find Z and to spend his final years in the deep, dark Amazon? Although some have suggested this explanation, there is no evidence for it, and it has the air of make-believe.

Fawcett's DNA?

We add a contemporary tale that might have some connection to Fawcett—and is just too good to pass up. Fast-forward to March 2014: this is a true story. An airplane is flying low over a desolate area of the Amazon jungle, taking amazing pictures of startled tribesmen who most likely never had any contact with the outside world. They are painted with bright red and black vegetable dyes and have brandishing spears: others are shooting their poisoned arrows at the low-flying plane.

Photos show how excited and frightened they are to see, for the very first time, some loud noisy, drumming, threatening creature in the sky. The natives show their anger by jabbing their spears and taunting the strange, ominous enemy-intruder flying overhead.

The tribe, about two hundred in number, live on the Peruvian border in the Amazon basin: they are left alone to live in peace by the Brazilian government. Officials monitor the isolated tribe's living area to prevent encroachment by cattle ranchers, loggers, miners, and others who would put them at risk. Photos show that they have built and are living in straw-covered huts, which are surrounded by banana plants, corn, and peanut crops.

Is it possible that several light-skinned members of the tribe, which can be seen in the photos, might be descendants of Percy Fawcett? ("Startled Amazon Tribesmen Pictured Jabbing Their Spears as They See an Airplane for the First Time" 2014). We doubt it, but just maybe...

In the summer of 2014, Brazilian authorities were concerned when they learned that some members of an isolated Peruvian group in the Amazon might have been exposed to the flu. Since "uncontacted" groups are extremely vulnerable to diseases to which they have no immunity, Brazilian officials provided them with medical treatment for flu and flu vaccines (Gannon 2014).

In 2016, a Yanomami tribe of about one hundred people—living on the Brazilian side of the Venezuelan border and out of contact with the rest of the world—was startled to see a photographer and airplane flying low over their homes. It's estimated that approximately twenty-two thousand other Yanomami are living in similar communities in this general area.

According to author Gareth Davies,

Some of them can be seen wearing little clothing, leaning on sticks and appear to be staring in amazement as the photographer passed overhead. Yanomami shaman and activist Davi Kopenawa said: "The place where the uncontacted Indians live, fish, hunt and pant must be protected. The whole world must know that they are there in their forest and that the authorities must respect their right to live there." Davi, who is president of the Yanomami association Hutukara, has been called "the Dalai Lama of the rainforest." (Davies 2016)

The "Lost City" in the Honduras

It wasn't Percy Fawcett's "Lost City of Z," but archaeologists in 2016 were excavating artifacts from a "lost city" in Honduras in Central America—so sometimes lost cities can be found. And who knows what they will find tomorrow?

In 1526 Hernando Cortes, who was a Spanish Conquistador, first made reference to the site on one of his expeditions. Centuries later, in 2012, researchers found signs of ruins during an aerial survey of a remote region in the Honduras, which revealed evidence of a lost city. Then in 2015, a National Geographic team found the site and began excavating the area. They found a magnificent treasure of stone sculptures, which appear to date between 1000 and 1500 CE that have not been touched or seen since the city was abandoned.

The tops of many of these artifacts, which were shaped like a monkey's skull, were just protruding above the ground, and it's likely that others are completely buried. In 1940, Theodore Morde, an adventurer, pointed out that the city was known as White City of the Monkey of God. The name is derived from the white limestone rock in the region. He felt that the ancient civilization worshipped a huge simian deity represented by a statue.

It was said that Honduran Indians told Morde that the city's Monkey God fathered half-human children in the jungle. Morde, who supposedly found the site, never revealed its location and later committed suicide.

In January 2016 archaeologists have studied the area carefully and have unearthed jars, bowl, ceramic objects, and other artifacts. One vessel had vulture-shaped handles, a tray with a jaguar's head, and a throne carved with another jaguar. Other vessels were decorated with snakes, vultures, and zoomorphic (having or representing animal forms or gods of animal form) figures. Christopher Fisher, a Mesoamerican archaeologist on the team from Colorado State University, described an unusual object peeking above the ground as the head of "a were-jaguar," probably depicting a shaman in a transformed, spirit state.

It's an incredible story: researchers have found an unidentified civilization in the depths of the rain forest in Central America. While it's an amazing discovery of an abandoned city, it is also a vanished culture.

For five centuries the deserted city has lain untouched. But what happened to that mysterious civilization since no outsiders ever reached that remote region in the jungle? Was it a disease that wiped out the city—most likely (Mezzofiore 2016).

Come Out: The War Is Over

It was December 26, 1944, when Lieutenant Hiroo Onoda, a Japanese army intelligence officer, was sent to the tiny island of Lubang, off the west coast of southern Luzon in the Philippines. His mission was to carry out guerrilla warfare, and under no circumstances was he to surrender.

Shortly after landing in the Philippines with a small contingent of Japanese troops, Onoda and three other soldiers were the only survivors following a battle with local troops, so they fled off into the mountains.

Just nine months later, World War II had ended, with the surrender of Japan—but not for Lieutenant Onoda and his companions. While leaflets were dropped informing them that the war was over, Onoda believed that it was Allied propaganda.

For years they ate bananas, coconuts, and whatever else they could find to survive. In 1950, one of the soldiers surrendered, another was shot by a search party in 1954, and the third was killed by local police in 1972. Onoda, the lone survivor and now all alone, cautiously evaded search parties. For nearly thirty years, he survived playing "Catch Me if You Can." Onoda felt that he was doing his duty as a good soldier, carrying out his assigned orders.

Onoda Handing over His Sword

In February 1974, Norio Suzuki, a Japanese world traveler, found Onoda after searching the jungle for three days. Onoda, however, still refused to surrender saying that he was waiting for orders from his commanding officer. Suzuki returned to Japan and contacted Onoda's superior officer Major Yoshimi Taniguchi, who was a bookseller. In March, Major Taniguchi flew to the Philippines to cancel Onoda orders in person: he was finally relieved of his duty. Onoda then surrendered to Philippine president Ferdinand Marcos, handing over his Samurai sword. While he received a pardon from the Philippine government, many in Lubang did not forgive him for the people he killed during the time he was on the island.

When Onoda returned to Japan, he refused to accept the back pay the government offered him. When well-wishers presented him with money, he donated it to Yasukuni Shrine. Furthermore, he did not appear to be happy about being the center of attention and what he also viewed as the fading of traditional Japanese values.

In 1975, he left for Brazil, where he raised cattle. When he learned that a Japanese teenager in 1980 had murdered his parents, he returned to Japan. He then established the Onoda Nature School, which was an educational camp for young people: the camp was held at various locations throughout Japan.

Then in 1996, he finally decided to visit Lubang Island—the jungle that was his home for decades. He donated the equivalent of $10,000 for the local school.

For a period of time he spent several months each year in Brazil. In 2004, the Brazilian Air Force awarded him the Merit medal of Santos-Dumont. And in 2010, the Legislative Assembly of Mato Grosso do Sul presented him the title "Citizen of Mato Grosso do Sul."

Onoda continued to be associated with the revisionist organization Nippon Kaigi, which promoted the restoration of the administrative power of the monarchy and militarism in Japan. He died from pneumonia complications on January 16, 2014, at St. Luke's International Hospital in Tokyo ("Hiroo Onoda," *Wikipedia*).

The Jungle Is My Home

Off to See His Mom

David Good is off to see his mom, who lives in another country—hardly that unusual. While his dad is an American, his mom, whom he has not seen in twenty years, is a member of the Yanomami tribe in Venezuela and lives in a remote village in the Amazon jungle.

The Yanomami have no electricity, no plumbing, no medicine, and no currency. And they have no written language, so they have no written word for "love." What's more, they have no counting system. A single bird is one, and a pair of birds is two: after that—it's many.

That was the world David was entering as he approached the village deep in the Amazon, where his mom, Yarima, lived.

How David Came to Be

In 1975, David's father, Kenneth, who was an anthropology student, made his first trip to the Amazon. He made so many visits to the Yanomami tribe that they began to feel that he was one of them.

In 1978, the leader of the village offered him Yarima as his wife: she was no more than twelve years old. There was no wedding ceremony— the Yanomami don't have what we call marriage—but the arrangement was consummated. (Anthropologists—as one of Chris's colleagues who is an anthropologist assures him—frown on this kind of thing today.) Kenneth said, "I brought Yarima home to my mother and she said, 'Jesus, it's one thing to study these people—but to marry one? What are you going to do with someone who can only count to 2?' I said, 'We'll work it out.'"

Kenneth carried out his unusual marriage, living part-time on his own in America and part-time with his teenage wife in the Amazon. During one of his absences, Yarima had been brutally gang-raped over a period of several weeks. He arranged for her medical care, and then in November 1986 she moved to the United States. Shortly afterward, they were married, and Yarima gave birth to David, their first son (Callahan 2014).

Yarima Arrives in the United States

Since the Yanomami believed that the forest they lived in just continued on and on, one could only imagine the bewildering world Yarima found herself in when she arrived in Pennsylvania by plane. It was a trip that took her from the Stone Age to the present.

Yanomami women went topless in the jungle, but now she had to learn how to get fully dressed every day. She was flabbergasted: automobiles resembled some crazy wild animals and elevators appeared to be some kind of magic. When she saw her full reflection in a mirror for the first time, she was shocked; she felt more comfortable when the mirrors were covered.

Yarima, however, did adapt rather quickly to her new world and shortly came to enjoy TV, cars, and airplanes; while it was magic, it was good magic. But most of all, she enjoyed shopping—not surprising.

There was one thing, however, that stunned and amazed her more than anything else. Food in the Amazon is scarce and never wasted. For Yarima—who ate grub worms, monkeys, and boa constrictors—the experience of walking into a supermarket with limitless amounts of food was incomprehensible: it was a world turned upside down. She was also fascinated with our restaurants; imagine a place where you had a choice of many different foods and also have someone serve it to you! (How would Yarima describe ordering a big Mac and fries to her people back in her native village?)

One year after David was born, Yarima gave birth to a daughter, Vanessa, while they were on a trip back to the Amazon. Three years later, another son, Daniel, was born (Kremer 2013).

Yarima Goes Home

In 1991, Kenneth arranged to take his family to the Amazon to do a documentary with National Geographic. Yarima, who had difficulty communicating with everyone in the United States other than her husband, now decided not to return to America; the jungle, after all, was her home. Kenneth then took his three children with him back to America, where they were reared. David was five years old at the time.

David now felt abandoned and began to resent his strange family background. When his friends asked about his mother, he would always say that she died in an automobile accident. And today, he says, "I didn't want my friends to know that my mom's a naked jungle woman eating tarantulas. I didn't want to be known as a half-breed. And it was my revenge; I was angry that she left me. So I just wanted to stick with the story that she was dead" (Callahan 2014).

David Finds His Mom

David was a good student, but he was constantly troubled by the thought that he was abandoned. One day when he was about ten years old, he saw a picture of his mom in a tribal exhibit while on a class trip to the Museum of Natural History—he was shocked. Not long afterward, when he was in his teens, he began to drink and then he dropped out of school.

At age twenty, he began to read a book that his father had written about his life with his mom. He then began to think about her in a different light: he started to read and learn more about the Yanomami culture.

One year later, he wanted to visit his mom and reconnect with her. His other two siblings, however, did not show any desire to reunite with their mother. It took David several years to raise sufficient funds to be able to visit the Amazon.

Mama—I'm Home

It is now 2011, and we pick up David, now age twenty-five, who has just arrived at the place where his mom lives, in an isolated village where they rarely see outsiders, let alone an American.

Even after twenty years, David said that he recognized his mom right away. She was wearing wooden shoes, little clothing, and wooden shoots through her face. He said, "Mama, I made it, I'm home. It took me so long, but I made it." (Callahan 2014).

Yanomami do not hug each other, so he simply put his hand on her shoulder; and then shortly afterward, they both began to cry. During the next several months while he stayed at the village, they expressed their desire for him to stay and live with them. At one point, his mom presented him with two pretty young girls. She said, "This is your wife and this is your wife. You're going to have children with them. David quickly and politely refused the offer by telling her that he had a wife back home waiting for him, which was not true." (Callahan 2014).

Then in 2013, David returned to the Amazon to see his mom. When he visits the jungle, it's potluck time: he eats termites, monkeys, grub worms, and armadillo. David said, "I really want to be Yanomami, I want to trek through the jungle like they do." (Callahan 2014).

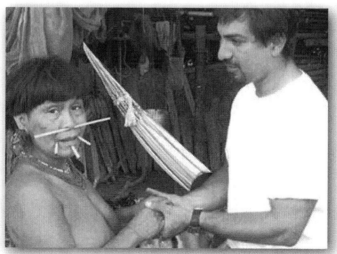

Yarima and David

As David is getting ready to leave the rain forest and return to America, Yarima said that she would like to visit the United State and see the rest of her family—hardly that unusual for a mom (Callahan 2014).

In 2013, David established The Good Project (TGP).

[It's] a nonprofit organization dedicated to the education, health care, and cultural preservation of the Yanomami and Cabecar indigenous groups in south and Central America, respectively. TGP is careful never to engage in any exploitative manner and is keenly aware of the sensitive balance between supporting social and economic progression while encouraging traditional values and customs and supporting their preservation. (The Good Project.com)

The *Maine*–Not So Well Remembered

Trouble is brewing in the Caribbean: the Cubans are revolting against four hundred years of Spanish colonial rule. It is 1898, and William McKinley, who is the twenty-fifth president of the United States, quickly orders our largest and newest battleship, the USS *Maine*, to leave Key West, Florida, and steam to Havana, Cuba, to protect our interests on the island. In that year, the United States formally annexes Hawaii. The Travelers Insurance Company issues the first auto insurance policy, Pepsi Cola is a new name for a carbonated drink, and Kellogg Corn Flakes is invented. And in France, Emile Zola is imprisoned for writing his "J'accuse" letter accusing the government of anti-Semitism and wrongly jailing Alfred Dreyfus.

Meanwhile, the mighty and formidable *Maine* arrived boldly at Havana Harbor on January 25: she remained anchored and was steadfast in the calm water of the harbor for three weeks. On a misty Tuesday evening of February 15, most of the crew on the *Maine* were resting and sleeping peacefully on board the ship. Suddenly, at 9:40 p.m., a massive explosion ripped through the forward section of the warship, and the *Maine* quickly sank to the bottom of the harbor; 266 men lost their lives.

Who sank the *Maine*? Was it a mine or was it an internal explosion? And who was responsible for the loss of our newest battleship? A number of investigations were carried out in an attempt to find out what caused the catastrophic explosion that destroyed her. There were no definite answers, only indefinite conclusions.

Over eleven decades later, even with modern technology, we are still unable to solve the mystery of the *Maine*. The haunting question lingers to this very day—was it sabotage or something else?

Background

The USS *Maine* was launched on November 18, 1889, at the Brooklyn Navy Yard. The *Maine*, however, was not commissioned until September 17, 1895. While it was viewed as a modern battleship, it was out of date by the time it entered service due to long delays in its construction, as well as the rapid changing technology in designing warships at the time. Nevertheless, the *Maine* was the largest ship built in a US Navy yard to date; it cost $2 million (equivalent to $53.2 million in 2016).

USS *Maine*

On November 5, 1895, the *Maine* was en route to Sandy Hook, New Jersey. The battleship then headed to Newport, Rhode Island, and also to Portland, Maine. She was then assigned to the North Atlantic

Squadron for maneuvers and fleet exercises, operating along the East Coast of the United States and also to the Caribbean.

On April 10, 1897, Captain Dwight Sigsbee took over as commander of the ship. Captain Sigsbee was anticipating only routine maneuvers in the Gulf of Mexico and was looking forward to shortly taking his new warship to New Orleans. But on January 24, 1898, President William McKinley ordered the USS *Maine* to Havana Harbor, Cuba, to protect US interests, since Spain was having difficulties with revolutionaries on the island. While it was the very first assignment for the glorious new battleship, sadly, it was also her last.

Prelude to the Disaster

By the late nineteenth century, revolts against Spanish rule by Cubans had been going on for years. The initial unsuccessful Cuban insurrection went on from 1868 to 1878 (the Ten Years War). Tensions between the United States and Spain developed during the attempts by Cubans to free the island from Spanish control, since we were supporting Cuba's liberation movement.

The second attempt for independence by Cuban revolutionaries began in April 1895. While Spain promised limited autonomy by 1897, the Cuban revolutionaries wanted complete freedom.

Spain sent thousands of troops to Cuba in an attempt to put down the rebellion. The harsh military action imposed on the Cubans eventually led to thousands of noncombatants dying of illness and starvation.

The deplorable action by Spain caused outrage and condemnation in the United States. Meanwhile, Spain was having political problems at home and was unable to carry out any meaningful reforms in Cuba. Nevertheless, Spain still wanted to control Cuba and maintain their national honor. The Cuban rebels, however, were a threat to Spain's power because they wanted total freedom. Jose Marti, the Cuban revolutionary, cried out, "Victory or the tomb." Tensions were rising on all sides—something had to give.

The Night the *Maine* Went Down

The *Maine* quickly left Key West, Florida, for Havana after President McKinley cleared the visit with an unenthusiastic government in Spain. There were riots in Havana earlier in January and the president wrote, "In view of the possibility of danger to American life and property, some means of protection should be at hand." Theodore Roosevelt, who was assistant secretary of the navy, enthusiastically approved.

The next day the *Maine* steamed into Havana Harbor and dropped anchor. While it was a friendly visit, rather than a confrontational one, the *Maine* was ready for any contingency. The appearance of the *Maine* in the harbor helped to assure the US citizens who were living there.

After several days, the atmosphere in Havana appeared to settle down. Captain Sigsbee, however, kept his crew confined to the ship, but they also were on alert watch. At the same time, there were the usual routine duties that the crew had to carry out while aboard ship.

That fateful Tuesday morning, February 15, 1898, was a day that was similar to the previous three weeks for the crew on the *Maine*. It appeared that its peacekeeping mission was over since Captain Sigsbee was scheduled to steam off for New Orleans for the Mardi Gras celebration in several days.

By 8:00 p.m., the officers were making routine checks to prepare for the evening security procedures aboard the ship. At 9:00 p.m., the bugler played Taps, indicating that it was time to turn in for the night: all is secure. The *Maine*'s clock sounded three bells for 9:30 p.m.—it would never chime again.

Just ten minutes later, at 9:40 p.m., two thundering explosions on board the *Maine* shattered the peaceful Havana Harbor. The forward section of the *Maine* was destroyed, and she slowly began to sink. Debris was flying all over the harbor, and it appeared likely that the death toll would be high. Tragically, most of the crew of 355 men were in the forward section of the ship when the explosions occurred: so there were 266 fatalities. Captain Sigsbee and many of the officers survived since they were quartered in the rear of the ship. America's newest battleship was now sitting on the bottom of the shallow harbor, although some of the damaged and dangled superstructure was still visible.

USS *Maine* on the Bottom

News of the sinking shocked the nation. While the United States did not go to war, the media gave the *Maine* sinking tremendous coverage. William Randolph Hearst, owner of the *New York Journal*, and Joseph Pulitzer, publisher of the *New York World*, both published fabricated and sensationalized stories to increase the circulation of their newspapers. Examples of American press headlines read, "Spanish Treachery," and "Destruction of the War Ship *Maine* Was the Work of an Enemy." War advocates shouted the rallying cry: "Remember the *Maine*" and "To Hell with Spain." The articles and photos did a great deal to arouse mass concerns in the United States for Cuba. As a result, the Spanish-American War is often referred to as the first "media war" ("USS *Maine* (ACR-1)," *Wikipedia*).

(The manner of publishing stories based on sensationalism and crude exaggeration by those newspaper owners was labeled "yellow journalism." The origin of the term illustrates the unethical tactics used by Hearst and Pulitzer. It all began when Hearst secretly hired Richard F.

Outcault, one of Pulitzer-prize cartoonists famous for his comic strip featuring "the yellow kid," to work for his newspaper, which caused a fierce rivalry between the two major newspapers. The rivalry soon got the public's attention, and that gave rise to the name "yellow journalism.")

More recently author W. Joseph Campbell wrote:

> An undying myth of American journalism is that yellow journalism, as practiced by William Randolph Hearst and Joseph Pulitzer, led the country to war with Spain in 1898.
>
> There is almost no evidence that the content of the yellow press, especially during the decisive weeks following the *Maine's* destruction, shaped the thinking, influenced the policy formulation, or informed the conduct of key White House officials.
>
> A significant body of research indicates that newspapers in small-town and rural America scoffed at, condemned, and ignores the exaggerated and fanciful reports appearing in New York City's yellow journals before and after the *Maine's* destruction. (Campbell 2010)

The Investigations
First Navy Inquiry

The US Navy immediately ordered an investigation into the sinking of the *Maine*. Captain William T. Sampson was selected to head up the board of inquiry. On March 21, the board submitted its official report to the Navy Department in Washington DC. President McKinley then submitted his report to Congress on March 28. At that same time, Spain released its own investigation into the sinking of the *Maine* to our State Department.

The Sampson Board stated that the crew was absolved of any negligence. They reported that there had been two distinct explosions, one following another. The initial blast occurred forward and slightly off to the port side and under the keel, forcing it upward at frame 18. According to the board, an exploding mine beneath the ship could only have caused the bending of the keel in that manner.

The exploding mine, in turn, caused the second louder and longer explosion of several forward magazines. The exploding magazines blew the *Maine's* superstructure upward and aft. The board did not speculate on who might have detonated the mine; they concluded that there was insufficient evidence to blame anyone for the destruction of the *Maine*.

When the board's report was announced, the American public reacted with outrage and the media also joined in, placing guilt on the Spanish government (Fisher 2009).

Spanish Inquiry

In 1898, the Spanish government commissioned two naval officers, Del Peral and De Salas, to investigate the *Maine* sinking. They concluded that spontaneous combustion from the coal bunkers, which were located next to the munition lockers, was most likely the cause of the explosion; other combustibles such as paint could also have been a factor.

They stated that if a mine caused the explosion, an upward spout of water would have been observed. Furthermore, no dead fish were seen floating on the water after the explosion. There was no evidence of a mine or any electric cables that might have been used to detonate a mine. Finally, they pointed out that munition lockers do not generally explode when a mine sinks a ship.

The results of the Spanish investigation were not reported at the time by the American press.

The Die Is Cast

The Die Is Cast (*Alea iacta est*) is a Latin phrase attributed by Suetonius, a Roman historian, to Julius Caesar in 49 BCE when he led his army across the River Rubicon in Northern Italy. The expression denotes that events have passed a point of no return.

After the details of the Sampson report and the Spanish inquiry became public knowledge, there was a sense of urgency in Washington to do something. While President McKinley was seeking a diplomatic solution to the Cuban problem, he was continuing to prepare the military for any contingency since it appeared more and more that we were at an impasse with Spain.

Spain, however, was steadfast in its desire to control Cuba. On April 11, McKinley requested permission from Congress to intervene; then on April 21, the president initiated a blockade of Cuba. (Not the last president to do so!) Two days later, Spain followed up by declaring war on the United States; and not to be outdone, two days later, on April 25, Congress announced a formal declaration of war with Spain.

(After the war broke out, Theodore Roosevelt resigned his position as assistant secretary of the navy and helped organize the first US Volunteer Cavalry Regiment known as the "Rough Riders." Subsequently, Colonel Roosevelt led his Rough Riders on a bold charge up San Juan Hill in the battle of San Juan Heights near Santiago, Cuba. He was eventually awarded the Medal of Honor posthumously for his brave rush up that hillside. He was the only president to receive the United States' highest military award for valor.

Other soldiers were also involved in driving the Spanish from the heights overlooking Santiago. One, not very well known then, was First Lieutenant John J. Pershing of the 10th Cavalry, who led an African

American regiment known as the famous "Buffalo soldiers." Less than two decades later, General "Black Jack" Pershing led the American Expeditionary Forces into battle in the fields of Europe during World War I.)

While the loss of the *Maine* did not lead to an immediate declaration of war, it served as a catalyst that eventually propelled us into a conflict with Spain. Four months later, the war was over and the United States took control of Puerto Rico, Guam, and the Philippines. We paid Spain $20 million (equivalent to about $574 million in 2016).

The Spanish-American War marked a significant change in US foreign policy. America moved toward a much more active role in international affairs, a trend that continues to the present day. The US victory over Spain, which had been a dominant power for four centuries, propelled America into the arena of world powers (Blow 1992).

The Second Navy Inquiry

For over a decade the shattered *Maine* remained helplessly on the bottom of the Havana Harbor, with some of its rusted and mangled steel superstructure protruding well above the surface of the water. Strangely, and somewhat ignominiously, over seventy bodies were still entombed within the forlorn warship.

Finally, in 1910, engineers began building a cofferdam around the wrecked *Maine*. The water was then pumped out so that the bodies could be recovered and buried. The procedure also provided access to the ship so that it could be examined in more detail, now that it was completely out of the water. The following year, President William Howard Taft, appointed a five-man Naval Inspection Board, headed up by Rear Admiral Charles E. Vreeland, to analyze the disaster and determine the cause of the explosion. Several members of the board were qualified engineers who were considered to be more competent to evaluate their findings than the line officers on the Sampson Board.

In 1911, the board concluded that an external explosion caused the ship's magazines to explode; however, the explosion was farther aft of the ship than reported in the Sampson Board report. Furthermore, they stated that the bending of the keel at frame 18 was due to the explosion of the magazines and not the result of an external explosion. In essence, the board concluded that a mine had detonated under the magazine, which caused the explosion that sank the *Maine* ("USS *Maine* (ACR-1)," *Wikipedia*).

Maine's Last Voyage

After the second naval inquiry, it was time to prepare the *Maine* for its final voyage. In mid-February 1912, after doing some necessary maintenance work on the ship, engineers poured water into the cofferdam until the *Maine* floated. The remaining sixty-six entombed bodies of the crew were placed aboard the cruiser *North Carolina*, which had entered the harbor.

On March 16, the tug *Osceola* then towed the *Maine* four miles out to sea escorted by the *North Carolina* and the light cruiser *Birmingham*. The *Maine's* sea cocks were then opened, the *Osceola* had cast off, and the *Maine* sank slowly.

With salutes from the escorting ships, the *Maine*—a ship to be remembered—sank slowly down six hundred fathoms (thirty-six hundred feet): down to her watery grave. As she was about to disappear from view, a bugler played Taps: Go to rest...go to rest.

A total of 229 crewmembers were eventually buried at Arlington Cemetery. The mast of the USS *Maine* was installed above a memorial in the cemetery to honor those who went down with her (Blow 1992).

The Rickover Inquiry

While the two naval inquiries concluded that a mine caused the *Maine* disaster, not everyone was in agreement with that theory. Lingering doubts and speculation for over six decades would not put the mystery riddle of what happened to the *Maine* to rest.

In 1974, Admiral Hyman Rickover, "Father of the Nuclear Navy," read an article titled "Returning to the Riddle of the Explosion that Sunk the *Maine*," by John M. Taylor in the *Washington Star-News*. Taylor claimed that the US Navy "made little use of its technically trained officers during its investigation of the tragedy."

Rickover became interested in the story and felt that modern technology might help determine the cause of the sinking. He called on two consultants who were experts on the effects that explosions have on ship hulls. The specialists had access to all the documentation from the two naval inquiries, in addition to information on the construction of the magazines and the *Maine* itself.

According to Dana Wegner, historical researcher and curator of Ship Models US Navy, who worked with Rickover on the investigation, numerous photos annotated by William Furgueson, chief engineer on the unwatering of the *Maine* in 1912, were also available for study. Since the photographs showed "no plausible evidence of penetration from the outside," the team reasoned that the explosions occurred inside the ship.

Rickover then concluded that there was no evidence that a mine sank the *Maine*. The report stated that the most likely cause of the explosion was due to spontaneous combustion of the coal in the bunker adjacent to the magazines: the coal fire heated the walls of the nearby magazines, causing them to explode.

In 1976, Rickover published his book about the investigation titled *How the Battleship Maine Was Destroyed*.

In the 2001 book *Theodore Roosevelt, the U.S. Navy and the Spanish-American War*, edited by Edward J. Marolda, Wegner offered additional information on the Rickover investigation.

Wegner pointed out that naval ship design and the type of coal used to fuel navy ships might have promoted the explosion proposed in Rickover's theory. Prior to the time that the *Maine* was constructed, ordinary bulkheads separated the coal bunkers (which used anthracite coal) from the ammunition storage compartments. The navy then switched over to using bituminous coal, which is much more volatile and releases large amount of firedamp that is explosive, which also supports the theory of spontaneous combustion.

Wegner also cited a 1949 study that showed a coal bunker fire, similar to what Rickover proposed, could have ignited the ammunition in the ship's locker ("USS *Maine* (ACR-1)," *Wikipedia*).

Other Investigations

In 1982, Louis L. Gould's book *The Spanish-American War and President McKinley* concluded that insufficient ventilation caused a fire in the coal bunkers, which in turn set off nearby gunpowder. In 1992, John L. Offner's book *An Unwanted War: The Diplomacy of the United States and Spain over Cuba* showed that from 1895 to 1898, there were thirteen other American ships that had fires linked with spontaneous combustion in coal bunkers. Offner, who did his doctoral dissertation on the Spanish-American War, was a colleague of mine for a number of years at Shippensburg University.

National Geographic Investigation

In 1998, *National Geographic* commissioned the Advance Marine Enterprises (AME) to investigate the destruction of the *Maine*. The AME results were based on computer modeling; however, their conclusions were inconclusive.

National Geographic reported, "A fire in the coal bunker could have generated sufficient heat to touch off an explosion in the adjacent magazine. On the other hand, computer analysis also showed that even a small, handmade mine could have penetrated the ship's hull and set off explosions within."

The investigation also concluded that "the size and location of the soil depression beneath the *Maine* is more readily explained by a mine explosion than by magazine explosions alone." The report went on to say that this did not mean it was definitely a mine that caused the disaster, but that it did add support to that theory.

Some team members from the Rickover investigation and some analysts from AME did not agree with the *National Geographic* conclusion. Wegner maintained that the *National Geographic* team was split between young members, who concentrated on computer-modeling results, and the older group, who relied on their own experience in evaluating photos of the disaster. Furthermore, he said that the AME data, which were used for its results, were faulty regarding the design of the *Maine* as well as its ammunition storage compartments. Wegner added that the participants in the Rickover study were not consulted until the AME's results were almost finished and too late to confirm the data used or to get involved in meaningful conversation ("USS *Maine* (ACR-1)," *Wikipedia*).

The History Channel Investigation
In 2002, *The History Channel*, which had photos, experts, and archival sources available to them, produced a documentary on the sinking of the *Maine*. They concluded that a fire in the coal bunker caused the explosion: the bulkhead gave way, which allowed the fire in the coal bunker to then spread to the powder compartment.

Sabotage
According to Edward P. McMorrow, the destruction of the Maine could have been caused by an act of sabotage: he cites two factions that might have been responsible.

The Cuban rebel minority could have sabotaged the *Maine* with a bomb or mine. Their reason for carrying out such a despicable act would be to get the United States to intervene on their behalf in their fight for independence—knowing that the Spanish would be blamed for destroying the *Maine*.

While the rebels wanted the support of the United States, blowing up one of our newest warships would most likely have resulted in the loss of many American lives. Furthermore, it could have ended up with the rebels losing American support for their cause. We feel that it's most unlikely the rebels would have resorted to such drastic action.

A second faction—a right-wing radical group—who favored Spanish rule and resented the United States for helping the rebels could have caused the explosion, which sank the *Maine*. Many Spanish army officers were part of a radical group of partisans who had served under the command of General Valeriano "The Butcher" Weyler y Nicolau.

Weyler, who had treated Cuban peasants horribly, was recalled for his actions by a new government that came into power in Madrid. His supporters—the Weylerites—were angered by his recall since they wanted Spain to continue as a colonial power. McMorrow wrote that the Weylerite radicals felt that the United States and the American press both, in part, were responsible for Weyler's recall and had a motive to destroy the *Maine*.

While it was possible for the radical group to blow up the *Maine*, they did not want to do anything that would cause the United States to intervene and support the rebels: they had too much to lose and little to gain. While the Weylerites had a motive—revenge—we feel that they would not have chosen to sabotage the *Maine* (McMorrow n.d.).

False Flag Theories

The term "false flag" is a covert operation designed to falsify the true identity of the attackers. Its origin comes from the days of the wooden sailing ships: one ship would fly a friendly flag to deceive the enemy before attacking. The Mukden episode in Manchuria in 1931, the Marco Polo Bridge incident in China in 1937, the Reichstag Fire in Germany in 1933, Nazi Germany in Gleiwitz near the Polish border in 1939, and the Winter War in Finland in 1939 were five false flags that were used to start wars.

Some have suggested that the sinking of the *Maine* was a false-flag operation carried out by the United States. This theory is the official view in Cuba. Cuban officials posit that the United States might have deliberately blown up the *Maine* to create a pretext for going to war with Spain.

In the 1920s, a monument was built in Havana to commemorate the sailors who died and to honor US-Cuban friendship. An eagle, the United States' national symbol, was placed on top of the monument. In 1961, Cuban Communist radicals, who were in control of Cuba, toppled the eagle from the monument, and the fragmented remains are proudly displayed in a museum. The wording on the monument describes the crew on the *Maine* as "victims sacrificed to the imperialist greed in its fervor to seize control of Cuba."

Eliades Acosta, Cuban historian, who heads up the Cuban Communist Party's Committee on Culture and is the former director of the Jose Marti National Library in Havana, stated in an interview with the *New York Times* that it is generally viewed in Cuba that the United States probably was responsible for the disaster. He then said, "Americans died for the freedom of Cuba and that should be recognized. But others wanted to annex Cuba, and that should be criticized." Mikhail Khazin, Russian economist, who stated in a 2008 Pravda interview "the Americans blew up their own battleship *Maine*," also advocates this theory.

Conclusion

In 1898, the Sampson Board of Inquiry was the first team to investigate the *Maine* disaster: they concluded that a mine destroyed the USS *Maine*.

About the same time, a Spanish inquiry reported that their study showed that spontaneous combustion was the most likely cause of the explosion. This theory did not, however, receive much attention since it was generally assumed that the US Navy inquiry was correct that an external mine sank the *Maine*.

Over two decades later, in 1911, the Vreeland Board's Court of Inquiry carried out a second navy investigation. While this study was more thorough, it also concluded that a mine was responsible for the *Maine* sinking.

And for over seven decades, it was generally believed that a mine device of some sort sabotaged the *Maine*. But in 1974, Admiral Hyman

G. Rickover began a private investigation of the *Maine* explosion. He concluded that the most likely cause of the *Maine* disaster was due to spontaneous combustion of the coal.

In 1998, almost twenty-five years later, *National Geographic* commissioned an investigation to look into the *Maine* disaster. They concluded that computer analysis, while not definite, supported the theory that the explosion was due to an external mine. Two books, which we mentioned earlier, also supported an internal explosion.

Then in 2002, *The History Channel* investigation report indicated that the explosion was due to a fire in the coal bunker.

As you can see, the seesaw battle continued on. There was support for both a mine as well as spontaneous combustion of the coal for the explosion that resulted in the destruction of the *Maine*. It's not exactly a flip of the coin to get it right, but it's close.

The cause of the explosion and a definite explanation for the destruction of the USS *Maine*, despite the efforts of the various investigating teams, remain a mystery. Nevertheless, we conclude that the computer analysis evidence, which supports the theory that an external mine of some sort is the most likely cause of the explosion, is correct.

The cause of the explosion of the USS *Maine* will most likely never be known with complete certainty—it will remain an unsolved mystery. But what happened on February 15, 1898, the night the *Maine* went down, is clear. The event was a compelling force that propelled the United States into the Spanish-American War. More importantly, it marked the emergence of the United States as a world power.

Aftermath

In April 1961, just three weeks after John F. Kennedy succeeded Dwight D. Eisenhower as president, the United States attempted to free Cuba from Fidel Castro's ironclad rule. The plan supported by the Central Intelligence Agency (CIA) namely The Bay of Pigs Invasion ended in pathetic failure.

By March 1962, the Cold War was heating up and a confrontation was brewing between the United States and the Soviet Union concerning Soviet ballistic missiles being deployed in Cuba.

Meanwhile, the military brass was still seething over the miserable failure of the Bay of Pigs disaster and was seeking revenge.

[A Cuban false-flag attack called] Operation Northwoods was conceived by the Department of Defense and the Joint Chiefs of Staff and presented to Defense Secretary Robert McNamarra by JCS Chairman General Lyman Lemnitzer on March 13, 1962. The plan called for various plots against American civilian targets, on the Guantanamo Bay Naval Base and U.S. mainland by U.S. government operatives.

It was an audacious—and diabolical—plan....It called for assassinations of Cuban emigres, blowing up a U.S. ship, staging terrorist acts in major U.S. cities, even going so far as blaming a potential space flight explosion—with John Glenn aboard—on Cuba.

The plan was to then blame Cuba for their irresponsible and deplorable actions, providing a reason for a major military operation against Cuba. When President Kennedy learned about the proposal, he was outraged and fired General Lemnitzer from the Joint Chiefs of Staff.

Operation Northwoods remained secret in the archives until 2001, until the publication of *Body of Secrets* by James Bamford (Chi 2015).

Abandoned or Not?

Ranger on the Rampage

A Rambo-like US Ranger is sent on a mission to investigate a small camp to determine if they are holding any American (POWs). He is dropped into a dense, forested area; then he carefully finds his way to the camp. The ranger is ordered not to engage the enemy, but to gather as much information as he can. After completing his mission, he will be picked up at a designated area and returned to his base.

When he sees how horribly the American POWs are being treated, he becomes enraged: from then on it's a one-man rescue mission instead. There are about twenty-five guards at the camp, but the ranger charges in and starts shooting and empties magazine after magazine (which seem never to run out of ammunition). Even though he is badly injured, he continues on and manages to kill all the enemy guards.

He quickly arranges for several helicopters to pick up and rescue all the American prisoners safely; he is the last one to leave the ground. But this is, after all, just fiction—and there really doesn't seem to be any good reason to think that American POWs were left behind in Vietnam or Laos.

So there seems to be no story left for us to tell. Nevertheless, we do have an amazing story—unlike the Rambo tale of Vietnam—that really seems to be true. American prisoners were left behind and abandoned—but in Korea and not Vietnam. And this is the tale.

Background

When World War II ended in 1945, the United States and the Soviet Union divided the Korean peninsula into two nations: north and south Korea.

On June 25, 1950, the Korean War began as a civil war, which started when approximately seventy-five thousand soldiers from the North Korean Peoples' Army, without warning, crossed the thirty-eighth parallel and stormed into the Free Republic of South Korea. The conflict soon became international when the Chinese and Soviets supported the invading forces, while the United Nations armed forces (mostly American) backed South Korea.

It was a difficult and bloody war. The conflict went back and forth across the original thirty-eighth parallel and then continued to an eventual stalemate. Peace negotiations dragged on and on: neither side wanted to appear to be weak.

Finally, a cease-fire agreement was signed on July 27, 1953. The war ended returning Korea to a divided status, almost the same situation as it was prior to the war.

The Korean War did not receive the same media attention as World War II or the Vietnam War. It was, however, famously represented in the massive television series hit *M*A*S*H*, which was set in South Korea, near Seoul. *M*A*S*H* featured a team of doctors and nurses who treated the wounded who arrived at the Mobile Army Surgical Hospital by helicopter, bus, or ambulance. The series ran from 1972 to 1983. *Goodbye, Farewell and Amen* still stands as the most-watched finale of any television series.

The Treatment of Prisoners

Atrocities against American POWs in the Korean War have sadly been well documented. In 1950, the North Korean Army captured a large number of South Korean soldiers as well as many American soldiers in their massive surprise attack. At that time, North Korea did not have any system to handle the POWs: their army just had collection areas. The

prisoners were forced to march from these crude assembly regions to camps, but in many cases they were in reality "death marches."

According to US Senate Report No. 848 on Atrocities, "American military troops were starved, beaten and tortured by their Korean and Chinese captors. Every rule set forth in the Geneva Convention was broken when thousands of Americans died at the hands of barbaric Communists in the Korean War" ("Atrocities Against American POWs in Korean War" 83rd Congress – 2nd Session, 1954).

During a six-month period from November 1950 to 1951, the mortality rate—which was due mainly to starvation—for US POWs was a staggering 43 percent. Many accounts from individual prisoners have also shown that torture and inhumane treatment was common. Later in the war, some POWs were subjected to mass-indoctrination in anti-American propaganda (brainwashing). Other POWs were recruited to repeat anti-American propaganda in signed statements and public broadcasts. This short segment is just a sample of the horror that American POWs had to endure during that conflict.

In 1953, Allen Dulles, who was the director of the CIA, authorized the establishment of the MK-ULTRA project. It was a morally suspect covert program, which converted humans into guinea pigs for research into mind-altering drugs.

When Director Dulles learned that the US POWs were subjected to mind-control procedures by their captors, he wanted to close the "brain-washing gap" that existed between the East and the West. According to Kim Zetter, a freelance journalist, the "CIA's Technical Services Staff launched the highly classified project to study mind-control effects of this [LSD] and other psychedelic drugs, using unwitting U.S. and Canadian citizens as lab mice."

MK-ULTRA also had plans to produce a "Manchurian Candidate"—that is, someone to be programmed to carry out an atrocious crime such as an assassination. As readers of a certain age will know, such brainwashing was the key plot element in the classic 1962 film *The Manchurian Candidate*, starring Frank Sinatra, Laurence Harvey, Janet Leigh, and Angela Lansbury.

The mind-control project became public in 1975 through the investigations by the Church Committee and Rockefeller Commission that were set up to look into government surveillance operations following the Watergate wiretapping scandal (Zetter 2016).

The conception of brainwashing—of POWs returning from captivity to aid foreign enemies—has always interested the general public. In 2012, author Mark Sauter wrote:

> U. S. governments records, many declassified after decades of secrecy, are finally revealing the real story behind the enduring meme. The records describe Chinese spymasters assigning intelligence and propaganda missions to returning U. S. POWs and sending them home to a Soviet-linked support network of collaborators from Middle America to Eastern Europe.
>
> Told to expect contact once back in America, the men were "to lay low for two or three years," and "prepare the way in the United States for progressives to come later," Army intelligence reported. (Sauter 2012)

We recommend anyone interested in this topic to read Sauter's detailed and compelling article.

The Armistice Agreement

In July 1953, several months before the end of the war, both sides agreed to exchange some sick and wounded prisoners: it was called "Operation Little Switch." While it was a good beginning, it did raise some serious questions about others who may have been in captivity and in poor health. Based on intelligence reports, US officials were concerned about future POW exchanges. In this story, we will focus on US POWs.

On July 27, 1953, after the Korean War dragged on for about three years, both sides agreed to sign an Armistice Agreement (AA). US Army lieutenant general William K. Harrison, Jr., representing the United Nations Command, and North Korean General Nam II, representing the Korean People's Army and the Chinese People's Volunteer Army, signed the AA at Panmunjom, Korea; however, South Korea and the Soviet Union did not sign the truce. After the historic document was signed, there were no comments from either signing party and no handshakes: the signing event took only eleven minutes. The agreement was not a peace treaty, but a cease-fire. The Korean War, which began over six decades ago, still has not ended.

South Korea was hopeful that a political conference, which was proposed in the AA, would eventually unify Korea by peaceful means. Unfortunately, as we now know, this did not turn out to be the case.

The language in the AA allowed for loopholes, which later led to confusion about procedures governing POWs. In addition, the matter of who signed the AA led to disputes about many issues—including POWs.

POWs Exchange

In early August 1953, Operation Big Switch, the exchange of remaining prisoners of war, got underway but came to an end in December. Further negotiations regarding other POWs held by both sides turned out to be very difficult and little got accomplished (like most negotiations with North Korea ever since).

Evidence for POWs

Were soldiers really left behind in North Korea? We sketch here the compelling account presented in the impressive investigative book *American Trophies: How US POWs Were Surrendered by North Korea, China and Russia by Washington's "Cynical Attitude"* by Mark Sauter and John Zimmerlee.

We will feature one of the major findings (MF) in their investigation and summarize the evidence to support their conclusion.

MF: "The Pentagon had substantial evidence US POWs remained under enemy control at war's end, but declared them all dead—even those last known alive."

> Newly declassified documents show that the United States knew immediately after the Korean War that North Korea had failed to turn over hundreds of American prisoners known to be alive at the end of the war, adding to growing speculation that American prisoners might still be alive and in custody there.
>
> The documents obtained from the Dwight D. Eisenhower Presidential Library and other Government depositories by a Congressional committee, show that the Pentagon knew in December 1953 that more than 900 American troops were alive at the end of the war but were never released by the North Koreans.
>
> The documents were obtained by the House National Security subcommittee on military personnel. Congressional investigators said much of the information was confirmed by a former military aide to President Eisenhower, [Lt.] Col. Philip Corso. (Shenon 1996)

In February 1954, the US Army made a documentary on "Red atrocities," which included an interview with General Mark Clark, who was recently retired from his assignment running the Korean War. Clark stated that the Communists still held US POWs and would "sell them back to us in the future for the Red's own evil purposes."

Clark also said that the Communists did not account for approximately three thousand Allied prisoners, almost one thousand who were Americans, whom they held captive at some time during the Korean fighting. He went on to say, "no question in my mind that the Communists still hold some of them." The White House took action and informed the Pentagon to delete Clark's comments before the film was shown across the country.

In March 1954, General Nathan F. Twining, chief of staff, United States Air Force (later he became chairman of the Joint Chiefs), wrote a letter to the director of the CIA requesting a covert operation to recover US prisoners still being held captive by the Communists. The CIA did not buy the idea.

When Yuri Rastvorov, a KGB lieutenant colonel, defected to America in 1954, Lieutenant Colonel Philip brought him to the White House for a debriefing. That report was kept secret until author Sauter found it in 1989. The report, which was eventually declassified in 1990s, was an important part of Congressional hearings. In the report, Rastvorov confirmed that US and other UN POWs were being held in Siberia and that the "POWs will be screened by the Soviets and trained to be illegal residents (spies) in the U.S. or other countries where they can live as Americans" (Real life Manchurian Candidates!). When Sauter and Zimmerlee submitted their request through the Freedom of Information Act (FOIA) for more information on the Rastvorov report, the agency turned down their request.

In their book *Soldiers of Misfortune,* Jim Sanders and others wrote in 1954 that Assistant Secretary of the Army Hugh Milton II sent the following memo to his superiors:

A further complicating factor in the [POW] situation is that to continue to carry these personnel in a "missing" status is costing over one million dollars annually. It may be necessary at some future date to drop them from records as missing and presumed dead. (Sanders and others 2012).

Lieutenant General Eugene Tighe Jr. was director of the Defense Intelligence Agency from 1977 to 1981. He stated that when he served as an intelligence officer during the Korean War he had seen reports that clearly left no doubt that Americans had been shipped to China and the Soviet Union.

Upon retirement in 1986, he headed up a Pentagon review of American POWs in Southeast Asia. The investigation concluded that Americans might still be held in Vietnam: his findings were important for the Korean War situation as well. Tighe stated that the Pentagon had a "mindset to debunk the intelligence they receive on POWs." He then went on to say, "Some people have been disclaiming good (POW) reports for so long it's become habit forming."

In 1990, Colonel Millard "Mike" Peck was appointed chief of the Defense Intelligence Agency's Special Office for POW/MIAs. Peck received the Distinguished Service Cross for his bravery in combat in Vietnam. He was also knowledgeable about Asian affairs and had a keen interest in the Korean War issue.

The following year, however, Peck resigned. In his resignation letter, he stated that the office was mainly devoted to busywork and did not pay serious attention to solving the POW scandal. According to Sauter and Zimmerlee, he called the POW office a "black hole," which the Korean War POW/MIA families had also experienced. He went on to say, "That National leaders continue to address the prisoner of war and missing in action issue as the 'highest national priority' is a travesty."

In July 1991, President George H. W. Bush mentioned to the press that he handed Mikhail Gorbachev, president of the Soviet Union, a note regarding POWs. According to Sauter and Zimmerlee, Bush said, "We raised that with the Soviets. They've maintained before and I would expect maintain again that they know of no America prisoners."

Family members and researchers were shocked and disappointed that the president would openly state that he did not expect an answer. Unfortunately, this pattern was repeated time and again since US officials often signaled their lack of interest in the topic. In fact, it happened again several months later when Boris Yeltsin was in the process of taking over as president of Russia.

Brent Scowcroft, US Air Force lieutenant general, served as the National Security adviser under US presidents Gerald Ford and George

H. W. Bush. In 1991, as National Security adviser to President Bush, Scowcroft (who as a White House official two decades earlier told families there was "no evidence" of POWs in China) now supported author Sauter in his fight to declassify the "[Lieutenant Colonel] Corso memo" regarding Korean War POWs in the Soviet Union.

Corso learned from interviewing Rastvorov that at least one trainload of four hundred US POWs went off to the Soviet Union. Corso said, "And I knew of other shipments." This information, which was written up, is referred to as the Corso memo. According to Jim Sanders and colleagues, in their book, *Soldiers of Misfortune*, Corso and C. D. Jackson, Eisenhower's chief national security aide, carried the written report to Eisenhower's office. Corso reported to the president as follows: "The conclusion was that Korean War POWs by the hundreds, perhaps thousands, had been sent to the Soviet Union." Corso pointed out that it was not likely the men would survive and that they were for all practical purposes dead. Furthermore, the Soviets would never admit having any prisoners. Corso recommended to President Eisenhower that the report be kept secret: he stated that Eisenhower agreed with the recommendation. According to Corso, "the report could never be made public and never was."

Corso was in charge of investigating the estimated number of US and UN POWs held at each campsite. At later hearings of the Senate Select Committee on POW/MIA Affairs, he provided firsthand testimony that hundreds of American POWs were left behind at those camps.

In 1991, Scowcroft wrote Congressman John Miller, a strong advocate for POWs, that his National Security Council staff denied the release of the Corso decades-old memo. It is of interest to note that the content of the memo contradicted current administration comments that there was "no evidence" Korean War POWs were retained or shipped to the Soviet Union.

Several reports cited by Sauter and Zimmerlee have been critical about US government goals for finding and identifying the missing from the Korean War, as well as other wars. The Pentagon has been unsuccessful in developing a unifying, accurate breakdown list of men who are POW, Missing in action (MIA), and Killed in action (KIA). Such incompetence and poor accounting has upset and disappointed family members. The United States has provided more than $1 billion in aid to North Korea—but we are still not getting an accounting for American POWs, MIAs, and KIAs in their homeland.

Air-force captain John Henry Zimmerlee disappeared over North Korea in March 1952: he was never returned to the United States. Author John Zimmerlee, his son, was discouraged and stymied by the limited information he was able to obtain concerning his father's disappearance.

Some years later, after continuing to be frustrated by the government's failure to declassify and correlate many files in the National Archives and other areas, he set up his own special database of Korean War cases. Family members from all over the country sought his help when they received little or no assistance from the government. Zimmerlee has provided information to over one thousand family members: we commend him highly for his dedication and excellent work. He is presently the volunteer executive director of the Korean & Cold War POW/MIA Network and board member of other POW/MIA groups.

According to Sauter and Zimmerlee:

> Widely-heralded executive orders from Presidents Clinton, Bush and Obama have also failed to open vast amounts of classified material, including that on POW/MIAs. We are still forbidden to review many documents older than we are. The process of getting them declassified can take years and even then produce heavily censored results, if the documents can be found at all.

Lest We Forget

A letter below from the Defense Intelligence Agency dated July 22, 2014, to Mark Sauter requesting information in 2012.

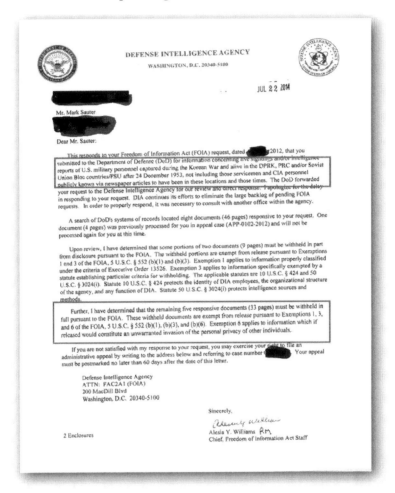

Some sentences taken from several paragraphs in the letter are shown below. The entire blown up version of this letter can be read on the Internet.

Second paragraph: A search of DoD's systems of records located eight documents (46 pages) responsive to your request.

Third paragraph: Upon review, I have determined that some portions of two documents (9 pages) must be withheld in part from disclosure pursuant to the FOIA.

Fourth paragraph: Further, I have determined that the remaining five responsive documents (33 pages) must be withheld in full pursuant to the FOIA.

("American POWs Kept Behind after the Korean War. What Happened to Them?")

More Stonewalling

According to journalist Michael Rubin, China is still not cooperating in 2015 regarding the resolution of several prisoner-of-war cases. He pointed out that there are two types of POW cases in which the Chinese officials refuse to share information:

> The first are prisoners held in official Peoples Republic of China POW camps in North Korea that were operated under Soviet advisers. There were specific Americans like Dick Desautels and Gerald "Jerry" Glasser, who were known to be alive in those camps but never returned or accounted for.
>
> The second were those Americans held in secret camps outside North Korea, in both China and—according to former Soviet officers, US reporting, and Russian inmates—in the Soviet Gulag as well. With very few exceptions, none of the Americans reported there by US intelligence during the war were ever returned. (Rubin 2015).

Rubin cited a number of instances that supports his contention that President Obama has only fast-tracked US-China cooperation and wonders why China deserves such cooperation when they stubbornly obstruct resolution of POW cases.

He concludes by saying, "To allow countries like China, North Korea, and Iran to avoid accountability for the hostages they have taken is to encourage further targeting of Americans in the future" (Rubin 2015).

The Families Have Waited Long Enough

(Memorial Day Weekend, 2016) The families of US aviators lost during spy flights near the Soviet Union, China and North Korea have fought for 80 years to learn the fate of their loved ones-some captured alive according to intelligence reports. Now time is running out for the aging wives and sisters of the missing, and they.ve grown tired of what they call indifference, stone-walling and secrecy from the US government. (Sauter 2016).

We believe the evidence shows that there were American POWs in the Korean War who were not returned. At the same time, however, North Korea, China, and Russia stonewalled and made it difficult for the United States to account for American soldiers whom they held captive.

Nevertheless, as Sauter and Zimmerlee pointed out, we also feel that the US government should be held to a higher standard, which it failed to meet. Sydney Schanberg, Pulitzer Prize winner, said, "For nearly a century now, our government has told us that when wars come to an end the return of American prisoners held by our adversaries becomes a matter of 'the highest national priority.' The evidence they [Sauter and Zimmerlee] have gathered makes Washington's denial of unreturned POWs seem ridiculous." (Sauter and Zimmerlee 2013).

The US government could have, and should have, done more to return missing Americans and also to recover the remains of those held captive after the Korean War.

Is Anyone Out There?

Late one night in the autumn of 1977, a huge radio telescope picked up an intriguing radio signal that had the potential to be the greatest discovery of all time—it could have changed the course of human history.

The compelling signal, which was seventy-two seconds in duration, came from a point in space in the direction of the constellation Sagittarius, far, far beyond our solar system. It was narrow and focused and came in at exactly the wavelength that an intelligent civilization might choose.

No one was present when the signal arrived on August 15: a receiver recorded the data and printed out the single pulse of radiation in a sequence of six numbers and letters. It wasn't until several days later when astronomer Jerry Ehman looked at the printout and saw what looked like a tantalizing trace of alien life. He quickly circled the signal and wrote "WOW" with a red pencil in the margin.

Whatever WOW was, it was transitory. While many attempts have been made, the source of the signal has never been identified, and it has never been repeated. But was it a communication from an extraterrestrial civilization?

After nearly four decades, the WOW still tantalizes us, and it hasn't been adequately explained. The signal, however, remains more than a curiosity: it is the strongest contender ever detected for an alien radio transmitter. One can only wonder where the signal came from and what's out there. But then, it's only a matter of time—or are we alone?

Speculation About Alien Life

Early thoughts on the plurality of worlds go back over two thousand years. The ancient Greeks debated the existence of life on other planets: Anaximander (610–546 BCE), who was a pre-Socratic Greek philosopher, led the way by speaking of infinite universes. Leucippus, Democritus, Epicurus, and other atomists then adopted his views.

Around 70 BCE, the Roman poet and philosopher Lucretius wrote this in his poem *De Rerum Natura* (*On the Nature of the Things*):

> Granted then, that empty space extends without limit in every direction and that seeds innumerable are rushing on countless courses through an unfathomable universe…it is in the highest degree unlikely that this earth and sky is the only one to have been created…So we must realize that there are other worlds in other parts of the universe, with races of different men and different animals. (Darling).

Teng Mu (1247–1206), a Chinese scholar of the Sung Dynasty, held similar views to the atomists. He wrote:

> Empty space is like a kingdom, and earth and sky are no more than a simple individual person in that kingdom. Upon one tree are many fruits, and in one kingdom there are many people.

How unreasonable it would be to suppose that, besides the earth and the sky, which we can see, there are no other skies and no other earths. (Darling).

Shortly before his death in 1543, Polish astronomer and mathematician Nicolaus Copernicus allowed his book *De revolutionibus orbium coelestium* (*On the Revolution of Celestial Spheres*) to be published. His book opened the door for many to think that other planets could also be inhabited like the Earth.

Decades later, in 1854, Giordano Bruno, a Dominican monk and philosopher in *De l'Infinito, Universo e Mondi* (*On the Infinite Universe and Worlds*) wrote: "I have declared infinite worlds to exist besides this our earth. It would not be worthy of God to manifest Himself in less than an infinite universe." It is likely, however, that Bruno was burned at the stake in 1600 for his religious beliefs rather than for his views on the plurality of worlds.

Then in 1686, the French scientist Bernard le Bovier de Fontenelle, who was a strong advocate for extraterrestrial life, wrote *Entretiens sur la pluralite des mondes* (*Conversations on the Plurality of Worlds*). It was an important work that described Copernican cosmology and the concept of many worlds, which carried over into the nineteenth century. It is considered an early significant work in the Age of Enlightenment.

While there was increasing interest in speculating about life on other worlds, it wasn't until over one hundred years later when various ideas were being proposed on how those on potential worlds might be contacted.

Searching for Extraterrestrial Intelligence

Carl Friedrich Gauss (1777–1855) was a German mathematician, astronomer, and physicist who published over 150 works. He is generally considered to be one of the greatest mathematicians of all time. His discoveries and writings not only influenced but also left a lasting mark in the areas of number theory, algebra, statistics, differential geometry, geodesy, astronomy, and physics, in particular, electromagnetism.

Gauss was one of the early proponents to recommend using equipment and other techniques in an attempt to communicate with life that might exist on other planets. He suggested using his surveying instrument, the heliotrope, to reflect sunlight out to the planets. Gauss also proposed cutting down lines of trees in a heavily dense forest in the Siberian tundra and then planting wheat or rye inside to form a giant right triangle, large enough to be seen from the Moon and Mars. He thought that the geometric figure and contrasting colors would convey the idea that it was a construction and not just a natural phenomenon.

(In 2015, thirteen-year-old Stephanie Virts sent a unique message out into space to her father, Commander Terry Virts, who was in the International Space Station 250 miles above the earth.

Hyundai used eleven sedans to craft her message in huge letters from the tire marks in the Delamar Dry Lake in Nevada. The message read:

The entire message was over two square miles and was seen clearly by her father who also took a picture of it (Gastelu 2015).

By the nineteenth century, astronomers were aware that Mars had some similarities to Earth. So it was only natural to assume that there might also be some form of life on Mars.

In 1869, French poet and inventor Charles Cros envisioned that the pinpoints of light seen on Mars and other planets were the lights of cities on those other worlds. He proposed that a large parabolic mirror could be used to focus light sources (electric lamps), which not only could be directed to Mars or Venus but also be turned on and off to send a message.

When Italian astronomer Giovanni Schiaparelli observed strange markings on Mars in 1877, he called them *canali*, which meant channels. When these *canali* were erroneously translated into English as canals, astronomers around the world became excited and speculation about life on Mars mushroomed.

About two decades later in 1896, Francis Galton, who was a British explorer and statistician, imagined that a light-based Morse code would be set up to communicate with the Martians. Galton was also aware that he couldn't assume that they had our base-ten counting system: maybe they didn't have five digits on each hand.

Even though those *canali* were later shown to be optical illusions, American astronomer and mathematician Percival Lowell in the early twentieth century still maintained that the canals were the works of an intelligent civilization. By 1909, astronomers at the Mount Wilson Observatory telescope in Southern California revealed that the features Lowell referred to were due to natural erosion.

At the beginning of the twentieth century, radio became a much more likely means of extraterrestrial communication since radio waves have less background noise and are also less affected by cosmic dust. It took decades, however, before radio was capable of focusing a beam out to a far off planet. Meanwhile, scientists were becoming more convinced that Mars was not suitable to support life and that they needed to search much farther out into space to look for presumed extraterrestrials.

Nevertheless, we thought we would include this short story about a radio broadcast that I (Harry) heard on Sunday, October 30, 1938:

It was the night before Halloween. I was fourteen years old.

I was sitting in our living room alone that night in the dark—we were not allowed to turn on any light fixture if it wasn't necessary—remember it was still the Great Depression—and the only light came from the small, dim orange-yellow light on the dial of the radio.

After turning on the radio and selecting a station, I heard an announcer on CBS national radio saying, "Good evening, ladies and gentlemen. From the Meridian Room in the Park Plaza in New York City, we bring you the dance music of Ramon Raquello and his orchestra."

Shortly afterward, the music stopped.

The radio announcer said in a stern tone of voice, "We interrupt our program of dance music to bring you a special bulletin from the Intercontinental Radio News." At twenty minutes before eight, central time, Professor Farrell of the Mount Jennings Observatory reports observing several explosions of incandescent gas, occurring at regular intervals on the planet Mars. The spectroscope indicates the gas to be hydrogen and moving toward Earth with enormous velocity.

The music resumes for a brief period.

The announcer interrupts: Here's the latest bulletin from the Intercontinental Radio News. It is reported that a huge, flaming object, believed to be a meteorite landed at Grover's Mill, in New Jersey.

Then, more music plays for a brief period.

The announcer: I have a grave announcement to make. Incredible as it may seem, both the observation of science and the evidence of our eyes lead to the inescapable assumption that those strange beings who landed in the Jersey farmlands tonight are the vanguard of an invading army from the planet Mars.

Now, there was no more music—only short pauses between excited news bulletins.

The announcer: This is Newark, New Jersey—Warning: poisonous black smoke is pouring in from the Jersey marshes.

The announcer, in a louder and more excited voice, shouted: the Martians are landing down all over the country.

The announcer: Smoke, black poisonous smoke, is drifting over New York City, and it has reached Times Square.

The announcer: People are trying to run away, but it's no use. The smoke is getting closer and closer now.

The announcer: This is the end. Isn't there anyone on the air? Isn't there anyone…a long silence follows.

After an hour-long series of shockingly plausible reports about invading Martians, an announcer said, "You have been listening to a CBS presentation of Orson Welles's dramatization of H. G. Wells' 'War of the Worlds.'"

It was estimated that six million people heard the fake radio broadcast. Surprisingly, almost two million people actually believed that a Martian attack was taking place. While there was no mass hysteria and widespread panic as has been reported, it was a scary night for me. In the beginning I was both curious and also anxious and then somewhat frightened toward the end of the program. All in all, it was a well-suited story for Halloween and also for retelling.

In 1950 physicist Enrico Fermi was discussing with his associates over lunch the possibility that many advanced civilizations might populate the Milky Way Galaxy. After a short while he said, but "Where is everybody?"

Fermi pointed out that since there are countless celestial bodies in the universe millions of years older than our Earth, there should be many, many civilizations out there and some should be much more advanced than ours. It's a paradox why we have not seen evidence of such civilizations—or, where are all the aliens?

Absence of a signal should never be used as a signal.

—JULIAN BIGELOW, 1947

Then in 1959, the search for extraterrestrial intelligence (SETI) got underway seriously when Giuseppe Cocconi and Philip Morrison published their paper "Searching for Interstellar Communication," which showed that radar transmitters were able to send signals many light-years out into space.

In the following year, American astronomer and astrophysicist Frank Drake performed the first observational attempt at detecting extraterrestrial communications in Project Ozma; he was searching for radio signals from two nearby stars. It was also the founding of SETI.

In 1961, he developed the Drake equation, which was a method that focused on the factors that determined how many intelligent, communicating civilizations are in the Milky Way galaxy. Drake suggested the equation could be used not to quantify the number of civilizations in our galaxy, but as a way to stimulate a discussion at the SETI meeting in that year. Nevertheless, in 2008 he estimated that the Milky Way might have around ten thousand extraterrestrial civilizations.

The Drake equation is a probabilistic argument. It is highly imprecise and unscientific, and the margin of error is beyond what might be considered acceptable. It is, of course, useful in that it summarizes all the concepts that scientists must think of when contemplating the big question of extraterrestrial life.

Did you know that a year after we landed on the moon, researchers picked up the first transmitted signal on Earth from another planet? The *Venera-7* was a Soviet spacecraft that was launched on August 17, 1970, as part of a series of probes to planet Venus. In mid-December, *Venera-7* landed on Venus and continued to send a weak signal for twenty-three minutes. It was the first spacecraft to communicate with Earth after landing on another planet. The transmitted data indicated something about the weather on Venus; its surface temperature was hot enough to melt lead or zinc, and the atmospheric pressure was around ninety-three times that on Earth, which is comparable to an ocean depth of approximately three thousand feet on Earth. (Surprisingly, giant whales manage to dive down that deep with ease and resurface easily.)

In November 1974, over 150 years after Gauss proposed his views on contacting alien worlds, Drake and other scientists constructed the very first message, which was sent from the Arecibo radio telescope into space: the scientists, however, are still waiting for an answer.

The message had a number system. The scientists' message included: (a) schematics of the DNA molecule; (b) a sketch of the solar system; (c) a diagram of the Arecibo radio telescope; (d) a sketch of a human being; (e) the population of Earth; and (f) a solar sketch of Earth showing where we live.

On August 20, 1977, just several days after astronomer Ehman spotted the WOW signal, *Voyager 2* blasted off into space. Then on September 5, *Voyager 1* followed; however, both are heading in different directions, and neither one is heading in the direction of a particular star. Both probes carried a message on a phonograph record—a twelve-inch gold-plated copper disk—that contained sounds and images to show the diversity of life and culture on Earth. There are 116 images on the golden disc. One can only wonder if some alien sometime in the distant future plays the record and hears Chuck Berry's "Johnny B. Goode"—what will he think? On the other hand the disc contains Beethoven's Fifth Symphony.

By August 2016, *Voyager 1* and its sister aircraft, *Voyager 2*, are about to leave the solar system after traveling for thirty-five years in space. *Voyager 1* is about 12 billion miles from Earth. It is farther out than any other spacecraft from our planet and traveling at around thirty-eight thousand miles per hour, moving away from Earth about 330 million miles each year. *Voyager 2* is not far behind.

While the National Aeronautics and Space Administration (NASA) continues to receive data from *Voyage 1*, it takes more than thirty-three hours to reach the spacecraft and get a reply. It's estimated that *Voyager 1* will have sufficient power to continue communicating with us until 2022 or maybe to 2025: after that, it will continue to wander the Milky Way. It will reach Oort cloud in around three hundred years and won't approach another planetary system for about fifty thousand years. But, will some alien ever read our message? (*"Voyager 1," Wikipedia*).

The WOW Signal

It was mid-August 1977: Jimmy Carter succeeded Gerald Ford as the thirtieth president of the United States; Led Zeppelin set a new world-record attendance for an indoor performance; the Bee Gees released the soundtrack to *Saturday Night Fever*—an all-time best-selling album; NASA launched *Voyager 1*; and Steven Spielberg's classic science fiction film, *Close Encounters of the Third Kind*, was released: it depicted a group of people who attempted to contact alien intelligence. (Chris denies authorship for any sentence that has both "Bee Gees" and "Led Zeppelin" in it.)

Only several months before Spielberg's sci-fi film came out, some scientists thought for a short while that they might have picked up a valid signal from an alien planet. It turned out, however, that almost everyone was paying attention to the shocking death of Elvis Presley—"King of Rock and Roll."

At that time in mid-August 1977, researcher Jerry Ehman was working with the Big Ear, a radio telescope operated by the Ohio State University as part of the SETI project. The WOW signal that Ehman circled was a very bright radio signal, which pulsed in at around 10:15 p.m. on August 15. The WOW pulse signal can be imagined to look like the following drawing.

The duration of the signal was seventy-two seconds (D) and the peak intensity (P) was over thirty times higher than the background noise level (B). Ehman was astonished at the signal's intensity and narrow range: after seventy-two seconds, it faded away. But what was it?

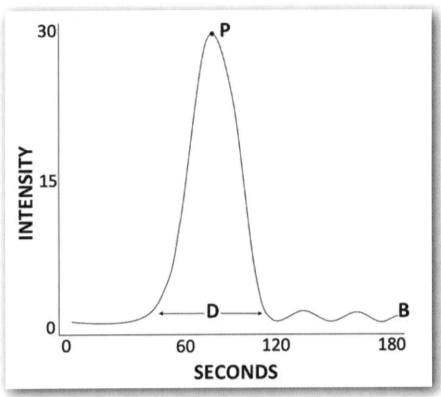

The WOW Pulse Signal

The signal came in from somewhere in outer space at 1,420 mega-hertz (MHz), which is the frequency of hydrogen. It's referred to as a "potential spectrum" in which terrestrial transmitters are not allowed to transmit since it's reserved for astronomical research.

So if you were an intelligent researcher who wanted to contact an intelligent researcher on another planet, you would use a frequency that you felt would likely be heard and also one that could be identified. Therefore, you would send a signal that could travel light-years with a minimum of background noise. You would most likely choose the spe-cial natural wavelength of hydrogen—the most abundant element in the universe—to send your message (Dunning 2012).

Amateur astronomer Robert Gray has studied the WOW for many years. In his book *The Elusive WOW: Searching for Extraterrestrial Intelligence*, he wrote:

The Ohio scientists looked for the signal on roughly a hundred subsequent days without finding it again, but their antenna could see that spot in the sky for only a few minutes each day so their efforts totaled only about four hours. John Kaus, the observatory director, published an account of the event in a scientific magazine of modest circulation, and the telescope returned to its survey for radio broadcasts from the stars.

In 2012, senior editor Ross Andersen at *Aeon Magazine* interviewed Robert Gray. We have summarized some comments and observations by Gray from that meeting:

(a) It's rather clear that the WOW profile was a radio signal and not a quasar or pulsar or another natural radio source.

(b) The signal came in at the frequency of hydrogen, which was significant because at the time that's the frequency scientists chose to listen to. Currently, however, researchers listen to millions of frequencies at a time and not try to speculate on which one an extraterrestrial might choose.

(c) The WOW signal most likely was not a computer glitch, because of the increase and decrease of intensity, which is exactly what an incoming radio signal would look like.

(d) Gray ruled out that the WOW came from space debris and thought it highly unlikely that it originated from a satellite. Then he went on to say, "The best way I can think to analogize this thing is to say that it was a tug on the cosmic fishing line. It doesn't prove that you have a fish on the line, but it does suggest that you keep your line in the water at that spot."

(e) Gray's favorite theory: If the WOW signal was from outer space, then perhaps it sweeps around its source the same way light flashes out from a lighthouse, which might explain why it hasn't reappeared.

(f) Some scientists are interested in a technique called optical SETI, where researchers are looking for sudden short flashes of light (much stronger than normal stars) with the idea that extraterrestrials are beaming a giant laser down at us.

(g) Gray pointed out that there is no way to tell if the WOW signal originated from a particular star or a group of stars.

(h) Gray talked about his experience working with the Very Large Array (VLA), one of the world's premier astronomical radio observatories located in New Mexico. It provides researchers with the ability to look at millions of objects across the sky. He said that as far as he knew, nobody has ever used the entire array to search for an extraterrestrial signal.

(i) According to Gray:

I've talked to a lot of astronomers and a lot of people involved with SETI…But I've never been able to find anyone who looked for it. In fact, nobody other than Ohio State seemed all that interested in trying to confirm it at all. Now fortunately that created a situation where I was able to convince several scientists to help me look for it using various kinds of radio telescopes, including the Very Large Array, the Mount Pleasant Radio Observatory in Tasmania, and the small one that I built myself. (Andersen 2012)

In 2012, the Arecibo Observatory sent a response containing ten thousand Twitter messages in the direction of the Sagittarius constellation. "In the response, Arecibo scientists have attempted to increase the chances of intelligent life receiving and decoding the celebrity videos and crowd-sourced tweets by attaching a repeating sequence header to each message that will let the recipient know that the messages are intentional and from another intelligent life form."

After a long wait—four decades—the mysterious WOW signal may soon be solved. Astrophysicist Antonio Paris of St. Petersburg College, Florida, found that two comets—266P/Christensen and 335P/Gibbs—were in the region of Chi Sagittarii star group the day that the WOW signal was detected.

Gigantic clouds of hydrogen gas surround the two comets, which were only discovered in 2006 and 2008, respectively. Recall, the WOW signal was the radio frequency that hydrogen naturally emits.

On June 25, 2017, comet 266P/Christensen will pass nearby Chi Sagittarii once again, and then on January 7, 2018, comet 335P/Gibbs will also pass by. Paris is planning to follow these events to determine if the WOW signal reoccurs.

Some astronomers, however, have expressed their doubts about Paris's hypothesis. We'll have to wait and see if the WOW mystery is solved or whether it will continue to remain as the best candidate for an extraterrestrial signal (Clark 2016).

The Search Goes On

In one of T. S. Eliot's Four Quartets titled "Little Gidding," he wrote:

> We shall not cease from exploration
> And the end of our exploring
> Will be to arrive where we started
> And know the place for the first time.

Since its inception in 1960, SETI has made significant progress. Recent discoveries have shown that there are countless numbers of planets that orbit other stars, and it's likely some of them are habitable.

Exoplanets are planets beyond our solar system: they come in all sizes and with varying distances from their parent stars. NASA is focusing on those that are about size of our Earth and are orbiting a sun in the habitable zone, that is, at distances, which could allow for liquid water to exist on its surface. In 2014, NASA Space Telescope discovered the first Earth-size planet orbiting in the habitable Zone, of a star outside our solar system, named Kepler-186f, which is about five hundred light-years from Earth in the Constellation Signus (Brake 2013).

In 2014, John P. Grotzinger, project scientist for the *Curiosity Rover*, reported new evidence that ancient lakes and streams had existed on

Mars millions of years ago. While it does not prove that life existed on Mars, the case that early Mars was suitable for life has grown stronger.

Recent discoveries have shown that there might be tens of billions of habitable planets in just our own Milky Way galaxy. These discoveries have added urgency to determine if we are alone in the cosmos.

Stephen Hawking, internationally renowned theoretical physicist, said, "There is no bigger question. It's time to commit to finding the answer—to search for life beyond Earth."

Starting in the summer of 2015, scientists are about to embark on a ten-year project, designated Breakthrough Listen—our biggest endeavor to search for alien life. Astronomers will be using the world's largest telescopes, searching the cosmos for civilizations beyond our solar system. They will be listening keenly for signals from millions of star systems closest to Earth as well as the nearest one hundred galaxies.

The project got underway with a $100 million from Russian billionaire Yuri Milner and is also supported by Stephen Hawking. Hawking stated that it's very likely simple life exists in other worlds, but intelligent life is an altogether different matter. And we on this planet need to pursue this endeavor to see if we are alone.

Peter Worden, one of the scientists leading the team, will carry out this research and attempt to determine whether signals they receive are natural phenomena or created by intelligent life. Keep in mind that radio signals take about four years to travel from Earth to the closest star outside our solar system, so any signals picked up by the researchers could have been sent many years or conceivably centuries ago.

What do you think? Will they detect a true WOW signal? (McBride and Hirschler 2015).

On September 28, 2015, NASA scientists reported that liquid water is still flowing seasonally on the surface of Mars. Researchers used an imager aboard the Mars Reconnaissance Orbiter to confirm their findings.

It is not evident, however, that life exists on the ancient planet now or has in the past. It does suggest that it's at least possible that there is a habitable environment on Mars today even though the discovered water is extremely salty. NASA scientists pointed out that they do not know its source, but they are following the water, hoping to find just simple living microbes.

Also in 2015, NASA found a "twin earth" dubbed Kepler-452b in the Constellation Cygnus. It's 60 percent larger than our Earth and has a 385-day year: it is also 1.5 billion years older than ours—and it orbits a sun in the habitable zone. Some scientists believe that it's possible life might have inhabited the planet. While it's a promising candidate, we need more data. It is, however, fourteen hundred light-years away and would take twenty-six million years to get there in a spaceship traveling at about thirty-five thousand miles per hour.

In that same year, scientists discovered the closest habitable planet outside our solar system, dubbed Wolf 1061c, which could support alien life. The rocky exoplanet, which was discovered by a team of astronomers at the University of New South Wales, orbits a red dwarf star, and it's only fourteen light-years away.

As of April 2016, Kepler has found more than one thousand confirmed exoplanets and over forty-five hundred candidate exoplanets since it was launched in 2009. Just one month later, Kepler and other methods have confirmed more than three thousand exoplanets—and the numbers continue to grow.

Then in August 2016, scientists discovered an "earth-like" planet, which is just outside our solar system and relatively close in space terms. The exciting finding is that its features suggest that it could support water. It is only 4.2 light-years away—but that's 25 trillion miles from Earth—and it would take a space probe until the end of the century to reach it!

By September 2016, China will be turning on the world's largest and most powerful radio telescope. The director-general of the Chinese Astronomical Society, Wu Xiangping, pointed out that the gargantuan telescope "will help us to search for intelligent life outside of the galaxy and explore the origins of the universe." They are hoping that if there is alien life out there in the cosmos, their super radio telescope will find it since their goal is to be the first nation to discover the existence of an advanced civilization.

Nan Rendong, who is the leading scientist on the project, said, "A radio telescope is like a sensitive ear, listening to tell meaningful radio messages from white nose in the universe. It is like identifying the sound of cicadas in a thunderstorm." (The Daily Galaxy via AP/Beijing 2016).

Space.com science writer Mike Wall wrote that numerous other planets in the universe probably hosted intelligent life long before Earth did, in a recent study by Adam Frank and Woodruff Sullivan. One cannot, however, conclude that there are many intelligent civilizations out there, waiting for us to contact them (Wall 2016).

Wall reported:

"The universe is more than 13 billion years old," Sullivan said... "That means that even if there have been 1,000 civilizations in our own galaxy, if they live only as long as we have been around—roughly 10,000 years—then all of them are likely already extinct. And others won't evolve until we are long gone. For us to have much chance of success in finding another 'contemporary' active technological civilization, on average they must last much longer than our present lifetime."

According to Kurzgesagt, we are limited to only a hundred-billionth of a percent of the observable universe, since dark energy is pushing the rest of the universe away from us at an incredibly fast speed. As a result, all matter outside of our local group will eventually move away from us forever. Kurzgesagt (German for "in a nutshell') is a Munich-based YouTube channel and design studio with a distinctive perspective on design and animation within the fields of education science and commerce.

Astronomers think that there could be billions of Earth-like planets in our Milky Way galaxy alone, suggesting that there surely must be life out in the cosmos somewhere. But that very huge number, as Paul Davies wrote, "is dwarfed by the odds against forming even simple organic molecules by random chance alone. The biggest uncertainty surrounds the first step-getting the microbes in the first place." So life in the cosmos might be more rare than we think (Davies 2016).

In October 2018, NASA is planning to launch the James Webb Space Telescope. It will have the power to look out across many light-years searching out the atmospheres of promising exoplanets, which are planets beyond our solar system. It will be able to reach the oldest and farthest stars in the universe. Scientists will be looking for "biosignature gases" (such as oxygen, water vapor, or industrial pollutants like ozone) on faraway planets that could only be produced by alien life, and the gold standard in biosignature gases is oxygen. While oxygen is an identification of life on Earth, it doesn't mean that it is necessarily true elsewhere. And where will it be, and what kind of environment will it also be when we finally first find life out there?

Some, however, will also be looking for necrosignatures—the remains of annihilated civilizations. And if they find evidence of a dead civilization, which destroyed itself or was eradicated by something else—what will it tell us? Will it be an omen for our own extinction—or will we learn from it?

By the end of 2018, a project called Messaging Extra Terrestrial Intelligence (METI) plans to send signals to a rocky planet circling Proxima Centauri, the closest star to the sun—4.2 light-years from Earth. According to science writer Lisa M. Krieger, "It would be the first effort to send powerful, repeated and intentional messages into space, targeting the same stars over months or years."

From time to time, it's likely some researches will be reporting strange signals they have detected and suggesting prematurely that it's a message from an extraterrestrial civilization. Understandably, many of these bold claims, however, will be due to an overemotional response to what they think they have seen. But, then, what astronomer does not want to be the first to make that audacious claim discovering intelligent life beyond Earth?

And we wonder what Galileo would think about these powerful telescopes that we have today?

Conclusion

Either we are alone in the Universe, or we are not.
Both are equally terrifying.

—Arthur C. Clarke

Since the various possibilities that the WOW had been generated by a terrestrial origin had been deemed improbable, we are left with the puzzling WOW signal. What was it?

While it looked like a duck and quacked like a duck, we still cannot say it was from an extraterrestrial origin. What we can say is that it was a radio transmission from space, which came from the direction of the Sagittarius constellation. And it remains the strongest candidate ever detected for an alien radio transmission, but the problem is that it has only been seen once. Perhaps, though, it might best be described as an interstellar radio source of unknown origin.

If the WOW signal came from extraterrestrials, then it's likely they were a remarkably advanced civilization, since their transmitter would have been vastly more powerful than anything that we have. Some civilization "way out there" could be so far ahead of us that they might view us as just simple organisms and of no value.

In an article on alien life, astrophysicist Caleb Scharf wrote: "If the Cosmos holds other life, and if some of that life has evolved beyond our own waypoints of complexity and technology, we should be considering some very extreme possibilities. Alien life could be so far advanced it becomes indistinguishable from physics."

While we haven't discovered alien life yet, we have, in a way, only begun searching seriously. The vast universe stretches out in all directions about 14 billion light-years: the 100 light-years our communications have traveled to date show that our signals have not journeyed very far out into the universe.

We do not think we are alone in the universe. The earth is just a tiny speck in the mind-boggling vastness of space. While we are located on the surface of a trivial-size planet, it is naïve to think that we who are positioned on an incidental section of just an ordinary galaxy should be unique and special—and that our little Earth is the only example of what can happen in the vast mystifying cosmos. We think scientists will discover evidence of past life elsewhere in one or two decades. After a half-century, it's likely they will find simple living organisms—not little green men. It will, however, take many centuries to find intelligent life, but it's only a matter of time. While it's a long shot, it might just turn out that the WOW signal was a space brother after all. When it happens, the discovery of extraterrestrial life will rank among the most important events in human history.

On the other hand, will scientists who are searching the cosmos for intelligent extraterrestrial life first find evidence of a civilization that has already become extinct by natural causes or self-destruction?

But then, other more advanced civilizations may also be searching for us using different technology, and maybe those distant cousins of ours will be robots. But, will they be friendly? Will they have a consciousness? They might also be micro-robots, which could even be deadly. And if they are superintelligent robots, then all bets are off.

On the other hand, maybe we are alone. If so, then what does the future hold for us? Some day in the future on just an ordinary day, we will no longer be the most intelligent things on the planet.

Will robots inherit the earth?
Yes, but they will be our children.

—MARVIN MINSKY

Bibliography

A Watery Grave

Crouse, Douglass and Mitchel Maddux. 2009. "Geetha Angara—Chemist Found Dead on Feb. 9, 2005." Northjersey.com. February 2.

Mueller, Mark. 2015. "Death in the Water Tank; Nightmarish Case Remains Unsolved 10 Years Later." February 8, 2015. Updated March 18, 2015. (http://www.nj.com/news/index.ssf/2015/02/death_in_the_water_tank_nightmarish_case_remains_u.html).

Mueller, Mark. 2008. "Accident or murder? Former investigator addresses water-tank homicide." February 29.

Prud'Homme, Alex. 2012. *The Ripple Effect: The Fate of Freshwater in the Twenty-First Century.* New York: Scribner.

2012. "The Lady in the Passaic Valley Water Tank." November 20. (http://morbidnewjersey.com/2012/11/20/geetha-angara-the-lady-in-the-passaic-valley-water-tank/).

True Crime Diary. 2006. "The Water Tank Mystery." March 29.

Tresniowski, Alex. 2006. "A Killer among Us." Murder, Real People Stories. March 20. (http://people.com/archive/a-killer-among-us-vol-65-no-11/).

The Uranium Bath

Cole, D. C. 1988. *Bocks Conspiracy: The Truth Behind the Mysterious Disappearance in 1984 of Fernald Nuclear Plant Worker Dave Bocks Has Remained a Deep, Dark and Even Deadly U.S. Government Secret. Until Now.* (Self-published).

"Dave Bocks: When a Nuclear Plant Employee's Remains Are Found in the Plant Furnace, Some Say It Was Suicide, Others Murder." Unsolved Mysteries. (http://unsolved.com/archives/dave-bocks).

Noble, Kenneth B. 1988. "U.S. For Decades, Let Uranium Leak at Weapons Plant." Special to the *New York Times*. October 18.

Shanker, Thom. 1988. "Ohio Asks U. S. to Shut Nuclear Plant." *Chicago Tribune*. October 19. (http://articles.chicagotribune.com/1988-10-19/news/8802080600_1_nuclear-weapons-rocky-flats-plant-energy-department).

Vartabedian, Ralph. 2009. "Signs of Renewal Hide Toxic Legacy at Fernald Uranium-processing Plant in Ohio." *Los Angeles Times*. October 25.

Ashley's Last Night Out

2015a. "Ashley Erin Ouellette—Her Killer Remains Free." Justice4Ayla Cold Case File. March 11. (http://justiceforunsolvedinmaine.blogspot.com/2015/06/ashley-erin-ouellette-her-killer.html).

2015b. "Ashley Erin Ouellette—Her Killer Remains Free." June 4. (http://justiceforunsolvedinmaine.blogspot.com/2015/06/ashley-erin-ouellette-her-killer.html).

Collins, Kate Irish. 2001. "Unsolved Murder Plagues Family, Friends." Keep Me Current News. February 24. (http://www.keepme-current.com/sun_chronicle/news/unsolved-murder-plagues-family-friends/article_fe9cdafc-404c-11e0-8e6a-001cc4c002e0.html?mode=jqm).

2001. "Couple Deny Responsibility in 1999 Death of Teen." *Associated Press.* March 15, 2001.

1999. "Saco Teen Strangled, Police Affidavit Reveals." *Bangor Daily News.* February 19.

2016. "Scarborough Police Appeal for Information in Cold-Case Killing of Ashley Ouellette." February 11.

Crime Watch Daily. 2016. "Teen Girl at Sleepover Found Strangled; Second Teen Missing after Claiming Knowledge." April 21.

Maine Forum. Katiesback. 2002. "Unsolved Child Murder: Ashley Ouellette." November 22.

She Left No Trace

s.v. "Barbara Newhall Follett." *Wikipedia.*
This page was last modified on 16 November 2016, at 15:41. (https://en.wikipedia.org/wiki/Barbara_Newhall_Follett).

Collins, Paul. 2011. "Vanishing Act—Barbara Newhall Follett Was a Prodigy Who Transfixed the Literary World—and Then Vanished." *Lapham's Quarterly.* January 1.

Stefan. 2012a. "About Barbara Follett." Farksolia. February 15. (http://www.farksolia.org/about-barbara-follett/).

———. 2012b. "To a Daughter, One Year Lost—from Her Father." Farksolia. June 7.

Cause of Death: Lynching

Aiuto, Russell. n.d. "The Lynching of Leo Frank." Crime Library. (http://www.crimelibrary.com/notorious_murders/not_guilty/frank/1.html).

Alphin, Elaine Marie. 2014. *"An Unspeakable Crime: The Prosecution and Persecution of Leo Frank. 21*[st] *Century.*

s.v. "Leo Frank." *Wikipedia.*

Oney, Steve. 2004. *And The Dead Shall Rise: The Murder of Mary Phagan and the Lynching of Leo Frank.* New York: Vintage Books.

Georgiainfo.com.n.d. "The Leo Frank Case."

Cause of Death: Firing Squad

Adler, William. 2011. *The Man Who Never Died: The Life, Times, and Legacy of Joe Hill, American Labor Icon.* New York: Bloomsbury.

Caplan, Lincoln. 2016. "Death Throes: Changing How American Thinks about Capital Punishment." *Harvard Magazine.* November–December.

Foner, Philip S. 1965. *The Case of Joe Hill.* New York: International Publishers.

s.v. "Industrial Workers of the World." *Wikipedia.*

s.v. "Joe Hill." *Murderpedia.*

s.v. "Joe Hill." *Wikipedia.*

"Old Letter Sheds New Light on Joe Hill Murder Case." *New York Times.*

Palazzolo, Joe. 2016. "Executions at 25—Year Low." *Wall Street Journal*. October 24.

2015 "Utah lawmakers vote to become only state to allow firing squad."

Fox News Politics –Associated Press.

Smith, Gibbs M. 1969. *Joe Hill*. Salt Lake City: University of Utah Press.

"Theory # 1—'Eye Wobble Wobble,'" Industrial Workers of the World—a Union for All Workers. (https://iww.org/history/icons/wobbly/1).

The Big Boston Heist

Boser, Ulrich. 2009. *The Gardner Heist*. New York: HarperCollins Publishers.

Carr, Howie. 2015. "FBI Solves Decades-Old Art Heist, Suspect Had Been Represented by John Kerry." March 29.

2014. "FBI Has Confirmed Sightings of the Gardner Article." *The Boston Globe—Associated Press*. May 22.

s.v. "Isabella Stewart Gardner Museum." *Wikipedia*.

Kurkijan, Stephen. 2015. *Master Thieves*. New York: Public Affairs.

———. 2005. "Secrets behind the Largest Art Theft in History." The *Boston Globe*. March 13.

Mashberg, Tom. 2015. "25 Years after Gardner Museum Heist, Video Raises Questions." *New York Times*. August 6.

Thomson, Jason. 2016. "Isabella Stewart Gardner Theft: Is the Massive Art Heist About to Be Solved?" *Christian Science Monitor.* May 3.

Ward, Bob. 2014. "FBI Has Confirmed Sightings of Gardner Artwork." Fox25/MyFoxBoston. Last modified June 4.

The Caper and the Collusion in the Castle

Cafferky, John, and Kevin Hannafin. 2002. *Scandal and Betrayal.* Cork, Ireland: The Collins Press.

Dungan, Myles. 2003. *The Stealing of the Irish Crown Jewels: An Unsolved Crime.* Dublin: TownHouse.

O'Riordan, Tomas. 2001. "The Theft of the Irish Crown Jewels, 1907." *20th Century/Contemporary History, Features* 9 (4).

Attorney for the Damned

American Rhetoric: Clarence Darrow—"A Plea for Mercy." (http://www.americanrhetoric.com/speeches/cdarrowpleaformercy.htm).

1925–26 "Darrow's Summations in the Sweet Trial."

s.v. "Earl Rogers." *Wikipedia.*

Farrell, John A. n.d. "Clarence Darrow."

———. 2011. "Clarence Darrow: Jury Tamperer?" *Smithsonian Magazine.* December.

2007. "Great Trial Lawyers from the Past—Earl Rogers." June 16.

Lindner, Douglas O. "State v. John Scopes".

———. 2007. "The Massie Trials: A Commentary."

s.v. "*Los Angeles Times* Bombing." *Wikipedia.*

Lukas, J. 1997. Anthony *Big Trouble: A Murder in a Small Western Town Sets Off a Struggle for the Soul of America.* New York: Simon & Schuster.

s.v. "Massie Trial." *Wikipedia.*

Mesereau, Thomas A., Jr. 2006. "Daily Journal: Defender Legendary for Second Sight, Sixth Sense." December 5.

s.v. "Scopes Trial." *Wikipedia.*

Smith, Jack. 1989. "Early L.A. Law: Earl Rogers' Life in and out of Court Was More Dramatic than Fiction." January 8.

Lost in the Amazon—Hunting for Z

Andrews, Evan. 2015. "Explorer Percy Fawcett Disappears in the Amazon, 90 Years Ago." History.com.

Davies, Gareth. 2016. "The Incredible Moment an Uncontacted Amazon Tribe—Still Untouched by Civilisation—Stare in Wonder at a Photographer's Plane Flying above Them." *Daily Mail.* November 17.

Fawcett, Percy, and Brian Fawcett. 2001. *Exploration Fawcett.* New York: The Overlook Press.

Gannon, Megan. 2014. "'Uncontacted' Amazon People Treated for Flu." *LiveScience.* July 24.

Grann, David. 2009. *The Lost City of Z.* New York: Doubleday.

s.v. "Percy Fawcett." *Wikipedia.*

Daily Mail Reporter. 2014. "Startled Amazon Tribesmen Pictured Jabbing Their Spears as They See an Airplane for the First Time." March 29.

The "Lost City" in the Honduras

FoxNewsLatino. 2015. "Lost City Found Untouched in Deep Honduran Jungle, Explorers Keep Location Secret for Now." March 3.

Mezzofiore, Gianluca. 2016. "Inside the lost Honduran 'White City': Excavation Work Begins Deep in Jungle Where Archaeologists Believe They Have Found the Legendary 'City of Monkey God.'" *MailOnline.* January 19.

Come Out: The War Is Over

s.v. "Hiroo Onoda." *Wikipedia.*

The Jungle Is My Home

Callahan, Maureen. 2014. "US Man Finds Lost Mother in Amazon Tribe." *New York Post.* May 24.

Kremer, William. 2013. "Return to the Rainforest: A Son's Search for His Amazonian Mother." *BBC News Magazine.* August 28.

"The Good Project." Serving the Cabecar and Yanomami people.

The *Maine*–Not So Well Remembered

Blow, Michael. 1992. *A Ship to Remember: The Maine and the Spanish-American War.* New York: William Morrow & Co., Inc.

Campbell, W. Joseph. 2010. "Yellow Journalism 'Juiced' the Appetite for War? Not Likely." February 18.

Chi, Samuel. 2015. "An Audacious Plan for War with Cuba." RealClearHistory. March 13.

Fisher, Louis. 2009. "Destruction of the Maine (1898)." Law Library of Congress.

McMorrow, Edward P. "Who Destroyed the USS Maine—An opinion." The Spanish American War—Centennial Website.

Department of the Navy. "The Destruction of the USS *Maine*." Naval History and Heritage Command. (https://www.history.navy.mil/ browse-by-topic/disasters-and-phenomena/destruction-of-uss-maine.html).

s.v. "USS *Maine* (ACR-1)." *Wikipedia.*

Abandoned or Not?

"American POWs Kept Behind after the Korean War. What Happened to Them?"ain (http://www.kpows.com).

US Senate Report No. 848 on Atrocities. 1954. "Atrocities against American POWs in Korean War." 83rd Congress, 2nd Session, s

Rubin, Michael. 2015. "China Must Come Clean on POWs." November 23.

Sanders, Jim, Mark Sauter, and R. Cort Kirkwood. 1992. *Soldiers of Misfortune: Washington's Secret Betrayal of American POWs in the Soviet Union.* Washington, DC: National Press Books.

Sauter, Mark. 2012 "'Manchurian Candidate' Was No Mere Fiction." RealClearHistory, October 30.

Sauter, Mark, and John Zimmerlee. 2013. *American Trophies: How US POWs Were Surrendered to North Korea, China and Russia by Washington's "Cynical Attitude."* Orcinus Solutions, LLC, and John Zimmerlee.

———. 2016. "What Happened to POWs in North Korea?" RealClearHistory. May 28.

Shenon, Philip. 1996. "U.S. Knew in 1953 North Koreans Held American P.O.W.'s." *New York Times.* September 7.

Zetter, Kim. 2016. "CIA's Obsession with '*Manchurian Candidate.*'" RealClearHistory. April 13.

Is Anyone Out There?

Anderson, Paul Scott. 2012. "35 Years Later, the 'Wow!' Signal Still Tantalizes." February 27.

Andersen, Ross. 2012. "The 'Wow!' Signal: One Man's Search for SETI's Most Tantalizing Trace of Alien Life." February 16.

Ash, Summer. 2016. "The Easy Way to Let Extraterrestrials Know We Exist." *Atlantic.* April 13.

Brake, Mark. 2013. *Alien Life Imagined: Communicating the Science and Culture of Astrobiology.* Cambridge: Cambridge University Press.

The Daily Galaxy—Great Discoveries Channel. 2016. "China May Be Earth's First Nation to Detect Alien Life—Poised to Flip 'ON' Switch of World's Largest, Most Powerful Radio Telescope." September 8. (http://www.dailygalaxy.com/my_weblog/2016/09/china-may-be-earths-first-nation-to-detect-alien-life-poised-to-flip-the-on-switch-of-worlds-largest.html).

Clark, Stuart. 2016. "Alien 'WOW!' Signal Could Be Explained after Almost 40 Years." *Guardian.* April 14.

Darling, David. The worlds of David Darling. Encyclopekia of Science.

Davies, Paul. 2016. "Maybe Life in the Cosmos Is Rare After All." RealClearScience. May 23.

Dunning, Brian. 2012. "Was the Wow! Signal Alien." December 25.

Gastelu, Gary. "Hyundai Helps Daughter Send Message to Astronaut Dad in a Big Way," April 14, 2015, FoxNews.com.

Gray, Robert H. 2012. *The Elusive WOW: Searching for Extraterrestrial Intelligence.* Chicago: Palmer Square Press.

"How Far Can We Go? Limits of Humanity." Youtube—Kurzgesagt—in a Nutshell. (https://www.youtube.com/watch?v=ZL4yYHdDSWs).

Krieger, Lisa M. 2016. "Scientists Plan to Send Greetings to Other Worlds." *Mercury News.* December 26.

McBride, Sarah, and Ben Hirschler. 2015. "The $100 Million Question: Are We Alone in the Cosmos?" *Reuters.* July 20.

Scharf, Caleb. 2016. "Is Physical Law an Alien Intelligence?" Nautilus. com (http://nautil.us/issue/42/fakes/is-physical-law-an-alien-intel-ligence). November 17.

Wall, Mike. 2016. "The Universe Has Probably Hosted Alien Civilizations: Study." May 5.

Wolchover, Natalie. 2016. "Scientists Debate Signatures of Alien Life." *Quanta Magazine*. February 2.

s.v. "Wow! Signal." *Wikipedia*.

Acknowledgments

Most notably, we are grateful to our family—Karen, Greg, and Dr. Arlene—for their encouragement and support.

We appreciate the help we received from Rick Kerr, Lieutenant Colonel (ranger) of US Army (retired), who did the map—Route of Fawcett's Final Exploration. Rick also solved any computer problem that Harry had.

Our thanks go out to Nick Kalathas for his continued support. His outstanding photographs can be seen on www.natures.moments.com.

We want to thank the following in the medical profession: Barbara Blazek, Au. D. US Department of Veteran Affairs, Palo Alto, California; Dean W. Clark, DDS—Palo Alto, California; Andrew Epstein, MD Urology—Palo Alto Foundation Medical Group; and Martin Pastucka, DDS—Pastucka Dental Associates, Mechanicsburg, Pennsylvania, for their interest in our book.

We thank Dr. Diane Spokus, College of Health and Human Development at the Pennsylvania State University, for her steadfast support.

We are grateful to Dr. Kirk Moll, Chair of the Library Department and Reference and Research Librarian at Shippensburg University, for his help.

We appreciate the assistance we have received from the following at the Shippensburg University Library: Susan Hockenberry, Diane Kalathas, Mary Mowery, Teresa Strayer, and Denise Wietry.

We want to thank Brandon H. Woltz, Geo-Environmental Studies and HelpDesk Technician at Shippensburg University, who did the drawing for the WOW pulse signal. We also thank Emily Maust and Andrew Corchado at Shippensburg University for their assistance.

Our thanks to the following, who have helped in one way or another: Kathy Brunie, Dwayne Burt, Louanne Burt, William Burt, Patricia Coia, Joann Grandi, Lucas Kalathas, Jessica Kalathas, John Kalathas, Janine Kalathas, Molly Kennedy, Carol Kerr (Col. USAR Ret.), John Kerr (Capt. USAF), Katie Kerr, Rick Kerr (Major USAF), Rachel Kerr, Cora Catherine Kerr, MaryCarolyn and Christopher Komes, Joseph McAndrew, Candy McAndrew, and Cleo Ridley.

A SPECIAL TRIBUTE

A time to remember the passing of Richard E. Kerr Sr., a Korean War veteran, who served his country and family so well.

Printed in Great Britain
by Amazon